The
MAILBOX®
The Education Center®

Phonics

MW01259403

THE BEST OF TEACHER'S HELPER® Magazine

Grade 1

The best reproducible activities from the 2005–2008 issues of *Teacher's Helper®* magazine

- Initial consonants
- Final consonants
- Word families
- Short and long vowels
- Digraphs
- Blends
- R-controlled vowels
- Diphthongs

Managing Editor: Lynn Drolet

Editorial Team: Becky S. Andrews, Diane Badden, Kimberley Bruck, Karen A. Brudnak, Pam Crane, Georgia Davis, Lynette Dickerson, Tazmen Hansen, Marsha Heim, Lori Z. Henry, Debra Liverman, Kitty Lowrance, Dorothy C. McKinney, Thad H. McLaurin, Sharon Murphy, Jennifer Nunn, Mark Rainey, Hope Rodgers, Rebecca Saunders, Barry Slate, Rachael Traylor

Reinforce and assess key literacy skills!

www.themailbox.com

ISBN10 #1-56234-912-0 • ISBN13 #978-1-56234-911-0

Printed in the United States
10 9 8 7 6 5 4 3 2 1

Table of

Phonics

Initial Consonants

Auto Repair
m, s, t 4
b, f, r 5
d, h, n 6
c, g, l 7
k, l, p 8
Review 9

Postal Service
d, f, m, r 10
n, p, t, v 11
b, j, k, s 12
g, h, l, w 13
Review 14

Frogs
b, m, r, s 15
g, n, p, t 16
c, d, f, h 17
j, k, l, w 18
Review 19

Final Consonants

Apples
d, l, m 20

Corn Bushels
k, p, s 21

Short-Vowel Word Families

Spiders
-ack, -ap, -at 22
-ell, -est 23
-in, -ip, -it 24
-ock, -op 25
-uck, -ug, -ump 26

Chicks
-an, -at 27
-am, -ap 28
-ag, -ig 29
-ack, -ock, -uck 30
-all, -ill 31

Short Vowels

Bear
a, e, i 32

Space
a, i 33
a, o 34
a, i, o 35
e, u 36
e, u 37
Review 38

Butterflies
e 39

Long-Vowel Word Families

Dinosaurs
-ail, -ake 40
-ain, -ate 41
-ice, -ight 42
-ide, -ight 43
Review 44

Skunks
-ail, -ake, -ate 45
-ail, -ain, -ate 46
-ice, -ide, -ight 47
-ide, -ight, -ine 48
Review 49

Long-Vowel Spelling Patterns

Sand Castles
ea, ee 50

Sheep
o_e, oa 51

Desert
a_e, ai, ee, igh, o_e 52

Seals
oa, o_e 53
oa, ow 54
ea, ee 55
ea, ee 56
oa, o_e, ow, ea, ee 57

Contents

Fish
- *a_e, ai* 58
- *ai, ay* 59
- *i_e, igh* 60
- *ie, i_e, igh* 61

Ducks
- *a_e, ai* 62
- *a_e, ai, ay* 63
- *ea, ee* 64
- *i_e, igh* 65
- *oa, o_e* 66

Short- and Long-Vowel Discrimination

Penguins
- *a* 67
- *e* 68
- *i* 69
- *o* 70

Desert
- *a* 71
- *o* 72
- *e* 73
- *i* 74

Consonant Digraphs

Beavers
- *ch, sh, th* 75
- *ch, sh, th, wh* 76

Fishing
- *ch, sh* 77
- *ch, sh, th* 78

Pigs
- *ch* 79
- *sh* 80
- *ch, sh, th* 81
- *sh* 82
- *th* 83

Jellyfish
- *ch, sh, th* 84

Initial Consonant Blends

Flamingos
- *sn* 85
- *st* 86
- *sn, sp, st* 87
- *cl, fl, pl* 88
- *br, fr, gr* 89
- Review 90

Fishing
- *sk, sp, st* 91
- *cr, dr, tr* 92
- *cl, pl, sl* 93

Beavers
- *cl, pl, sl* 94
- *cr, dr, tr* 95
- *sk, sl, st, sw* 96

Final Consonant Blends

Tigers
- *st* 97
- *st* 98
- *nt* 99
- *nt* 100
- *nt, st* 101

R-Controlled Vowels

Clams
- *ar, ir, or* 102

Dogs
- *ar, ir* 103

Pelicans
- Short *a, ar* 104
- Short *o, or* 105
- Short *i, ir* 106
- *ar, er* 107
- *ar, ur* 108
- Review 109

Diphthongs

Birds
- *oi, oy* 110
- *oi, oy* 111
- *ou, ow* 112
- *ou, ow* 113
- *ou, ow* 114

Answer Keys 115

Name______________________________

Tune-up Time

Circle the beginning letter for each picture.

Color by the code.

Color Code
m — blue
s — yellow
t — red
10
s m t
t s m
s t m
m s t
t s m
6
t m s
m t s
m s t
s m t

Name ____________________

Changing the Oil

Circle the beginning letter for each picture.

Color by the code.

r f b

f b r

b r f

r b f

f r b

b f r

r b f

5

f b r

Color Code

b — orange

f — green

r — purple

Oil

Name________________________

Tools for Bear

Cut.

Glue to match the pictures and the beginning letters.

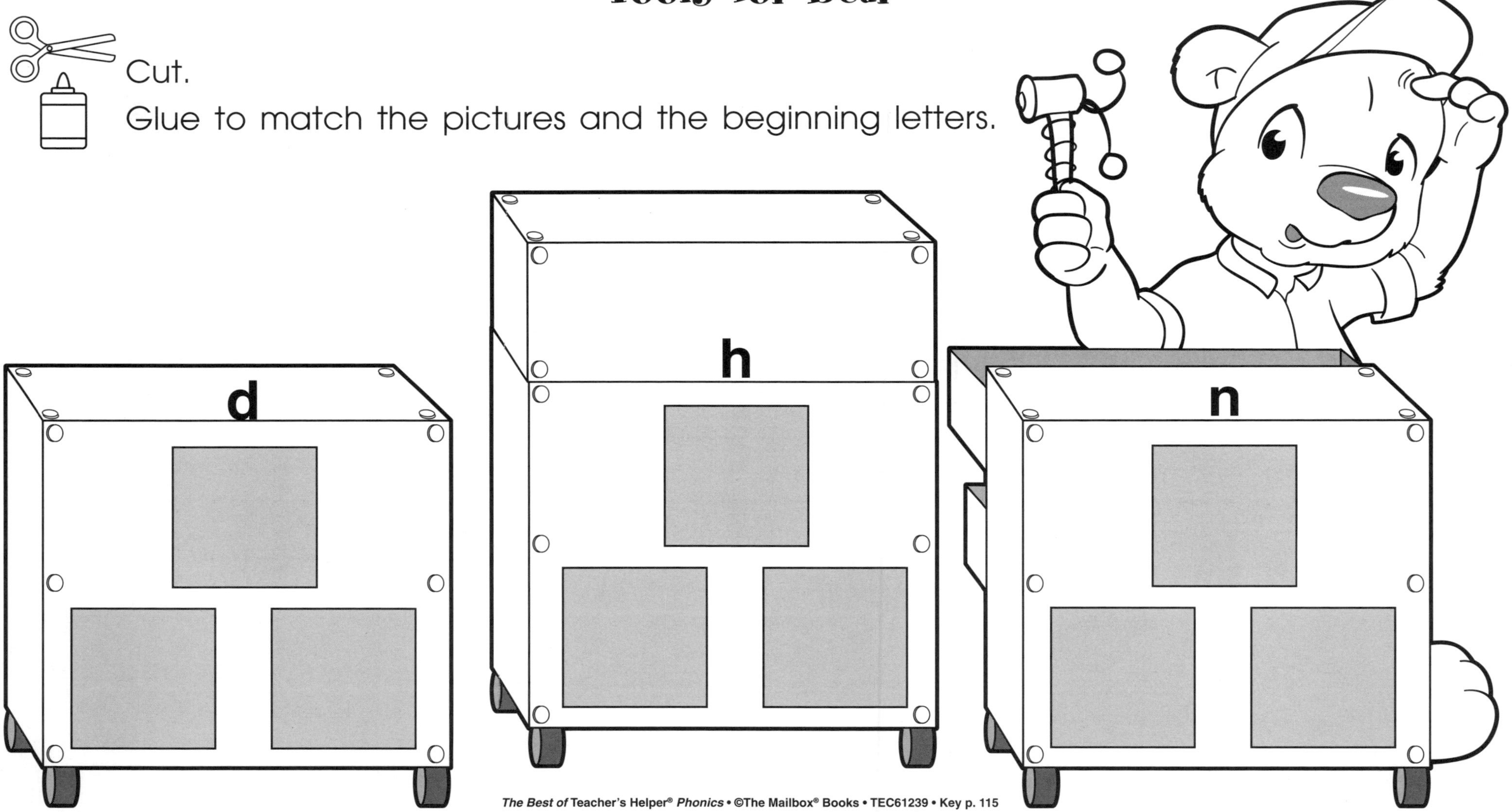

d

h

n

9

Name________________

Letting Off Steam

Write each beginning letter.
Color by the code.

__amp
__up
__irl
__eaf
__at
__oat
__ate
__an
__eg
Color Code
c — blue
g — green
l — orange

Name____

Car Care

Write each beginning letter.

Color by the code.

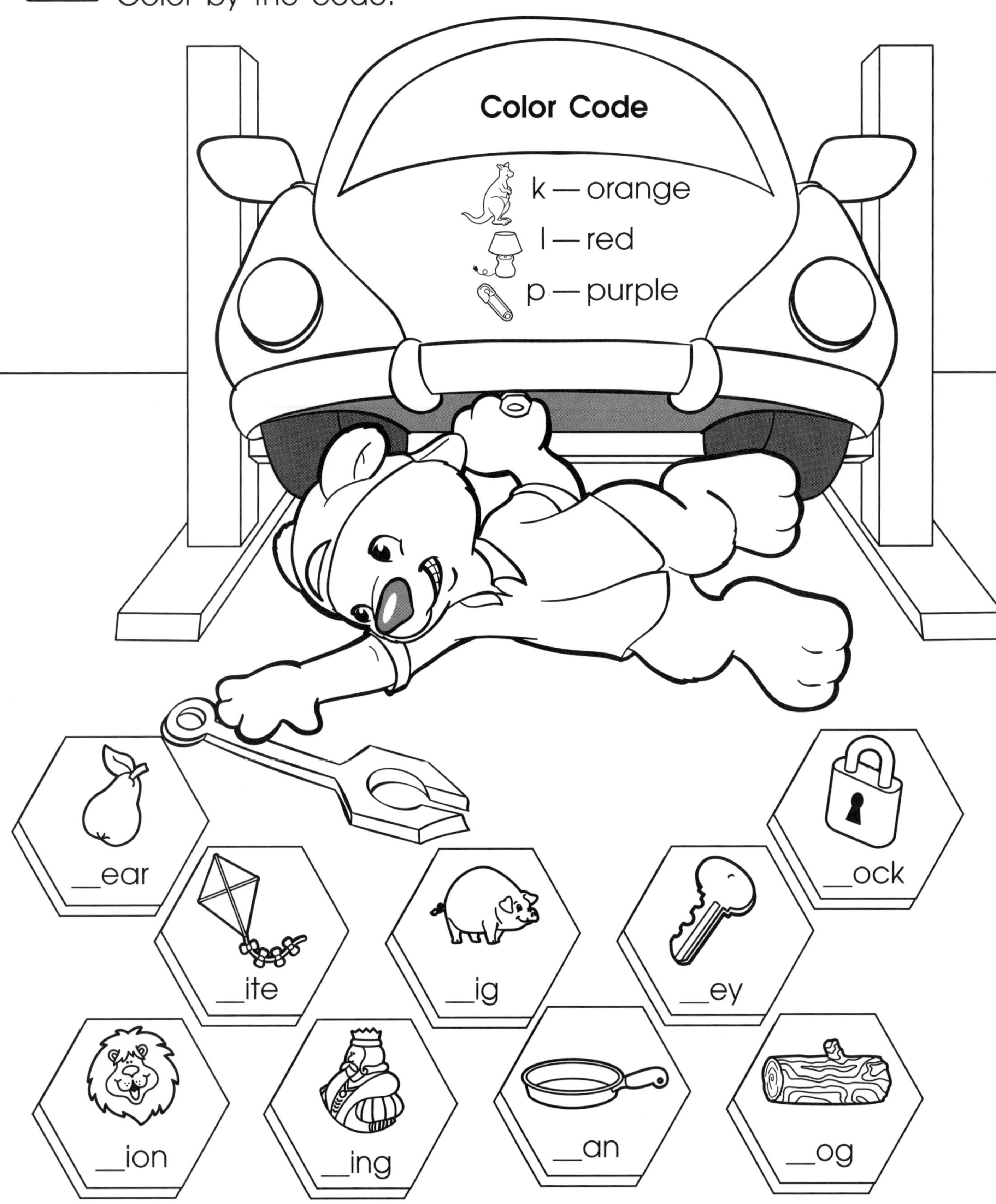
Color Code
k — orange
l — red
p — purple
__ear
__ite
__ig
__ey
__ock
__ion
__ing
__an
__og

Name________________________

Tires for Sale

Write each beginning letter.

Cross out each letter as you use it.

d h s n
m t l p
f r g c

__ouse

__ail

__even

__oot

__ake

__et

__op

__oll

__ift

__ay

__ake

__ip

Name____

Initial Consonants
d, f, m, r

Happy Notes

Cut.

Glue to match the pictures and the

beginning letters.

d
r
Dog
Raccoon

f
m
Fox
Mouse

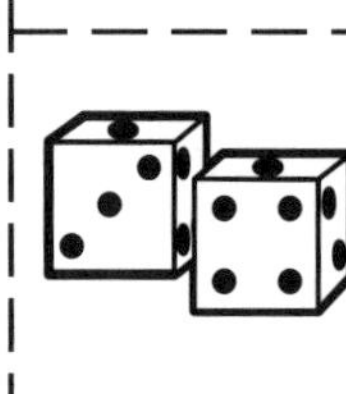

Name____

Mail Call

Circle the beginning letter for each picture.

Color the pictures by the code.

Color Code

n — yellow

p — blue

t — red

v — green

1.

p v t n

2.

v p t n

3.

p t v n

4.

n v p t

5.

n t v p

6.

v n p t

7.

p t v n

8.

n t p v

9.

v n p t

Name ______________________________

Gifts From Friends

Cut.

Glue to match the pictures and beginning letters.

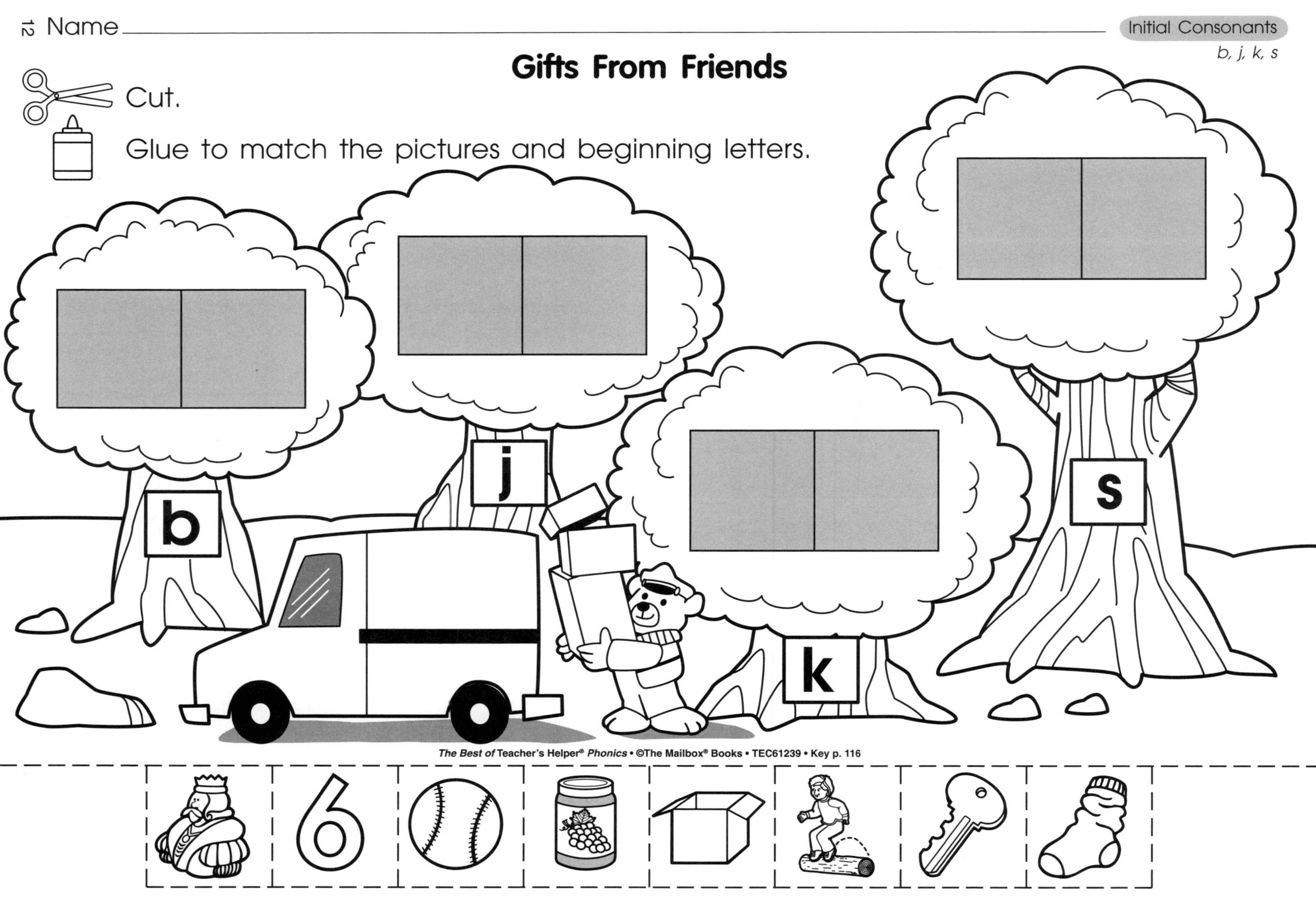
b
j
k
s

Name____________________

Daily Delivery

Write each beginning letter.

Color the pictures by the code.

Color Code
g — purple
h — orange
l — red
w — blue
____am
____eb
____oat
____and
____ig
____og
____ate
____eaf

Bonus Box: On the back of this paper, draw two more pictures whose names begin with *l*. Then write the word for each picture.

Name___________________________________

Initial Consonants
Review

Friendly Letters

Write each beginning letter.

1.  ____ive
2.  ____un
3.  ____og
4. ____ee
5.  ____ain
6. 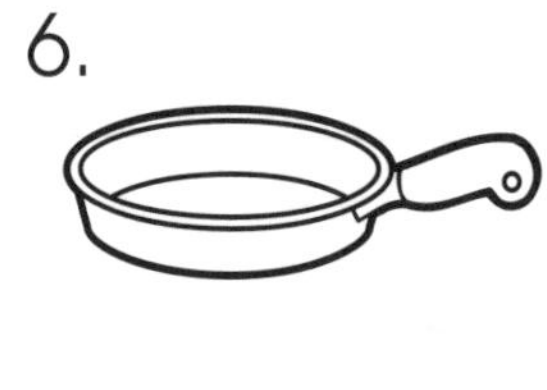 ____an
7. 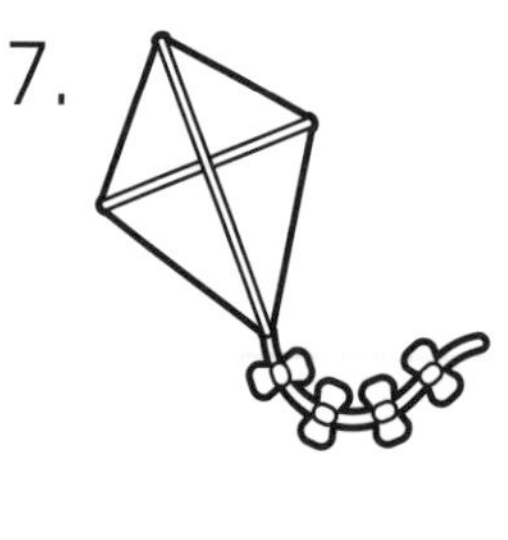 ____ite
8.  ____eb
9. 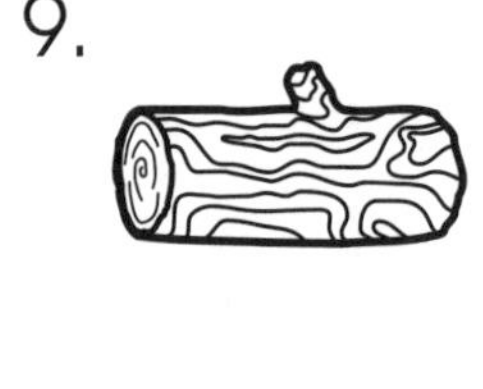  ____og
10.  ____ar
11.  ____ill
12.  ____ent

Name ___________________________________

Frogs on Logs

Cut.

Glue to match the pictures and the beginning letters.

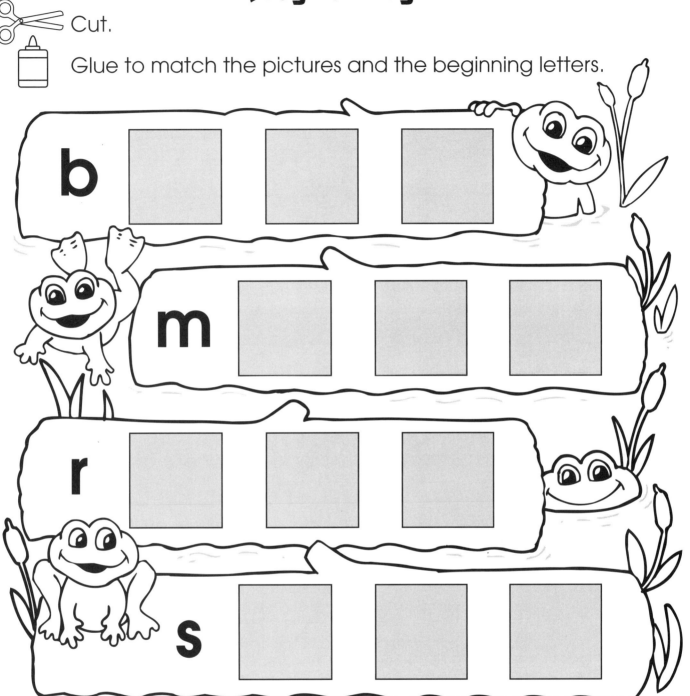

b

m

r

s

Name ______________________________

Lily Pad Leaps

Cut.

Glue to match the pictures and the beginning letters.

g

n

p

t

Name ____________________

Lily's Pad

Circle the beginning letter for each picture.

Color the lily pads by the code.

Color Code
c — blue
d — yellow
f — orange
h — red

1
c d f h
2
h f d c
3
f d h c
4
h f d c
5
d h f c
6
d c f h
7
f c h d
8
f h c d

Bonus Box: On the back of this paper, draw two more pictures whose names begin with *d*. Then write the word for each picture.

Name____

Initial Consonants
j, k, l, w

A Rocky Pond

Circle the beginning letter for each picture.

Color the pictures by the code.

1.  j k l w

2.  l w j k

3. 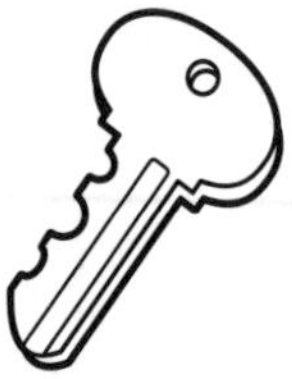 k l w j

4.  w j l k

5.  j w l k

6. 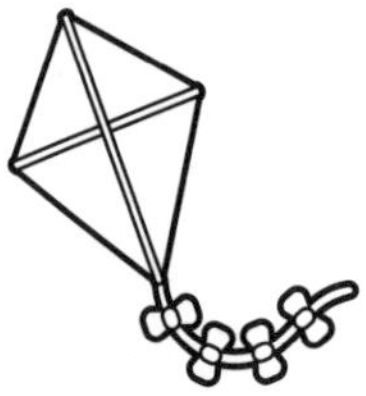 j w k l

7.  w l k j

8. l w k j

Color Code
j — yellow
k — blue
l — green
w — red

Bonus Box: Draw an X on the picture below whose name does not begin with *l*.

Name ____________________

Frogs and Flies

Write each beginning letter.

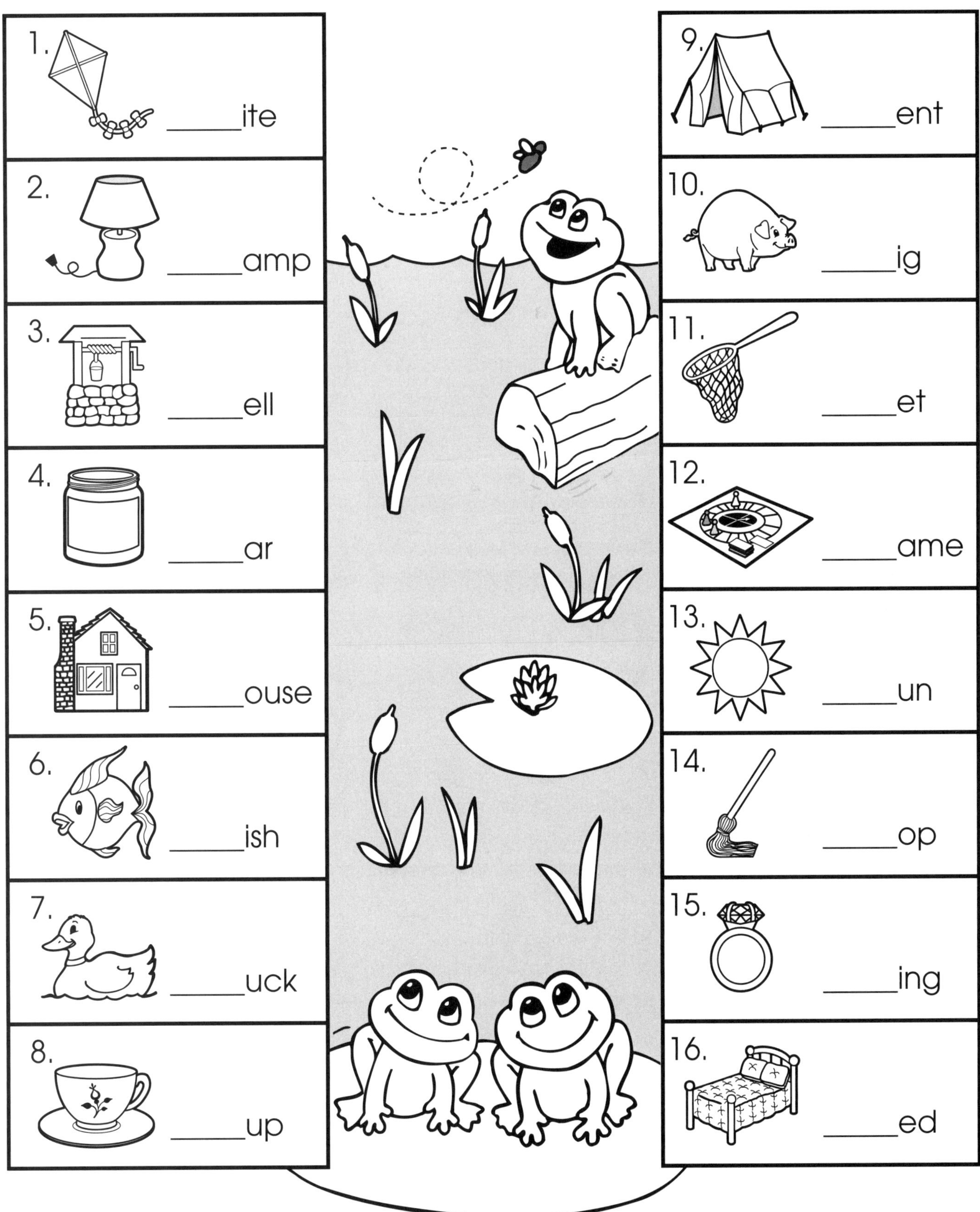
1.
____ite
2.
____amp
3.
____ell
4.
____ar
5.
____ouse
6.
____ish
7.
____uck
8.
____up
9.
____ent
10.
____ig
11.
____et
12.
____ame
13.
____un
14.
____op
15.
____ing
16.
____ed

Name_______________

Pick of the Apples

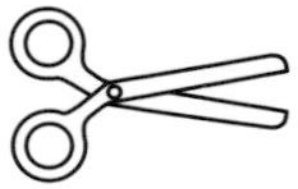

Cut.

Glue to match the ending sounds.

d

l

m

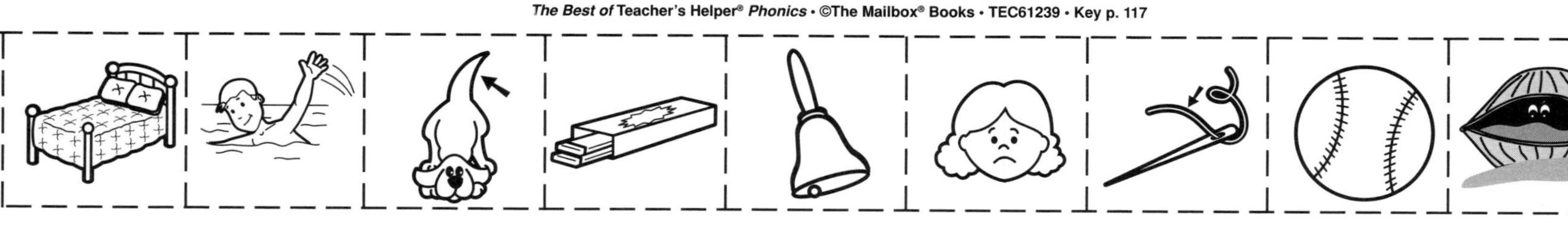

Name________________________________

A Hefty Harvest

Cut.

Glue to match the ending letters.

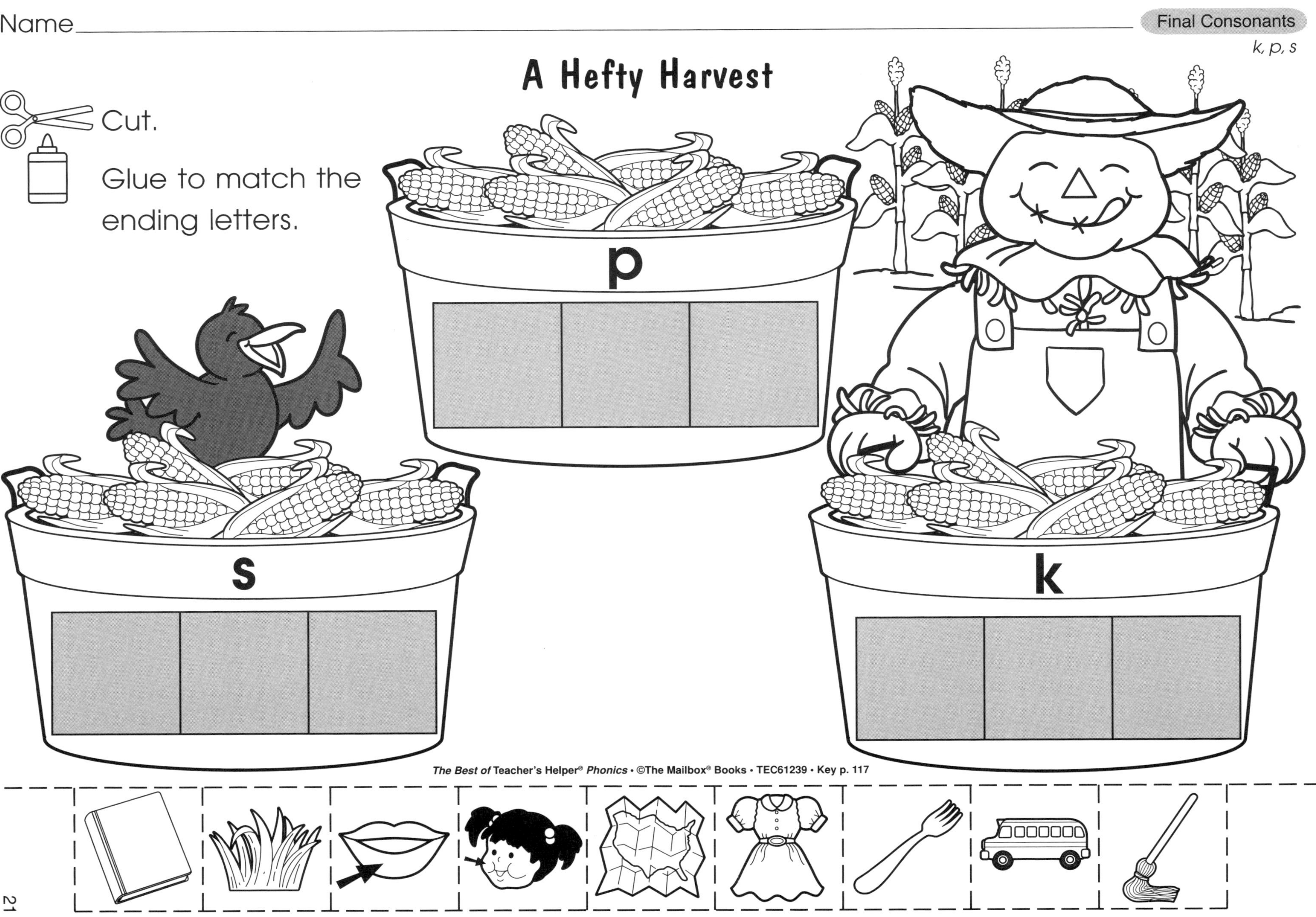
p
s
k

Name ____________________

Dropping In

Cut.

Glue to match the word.

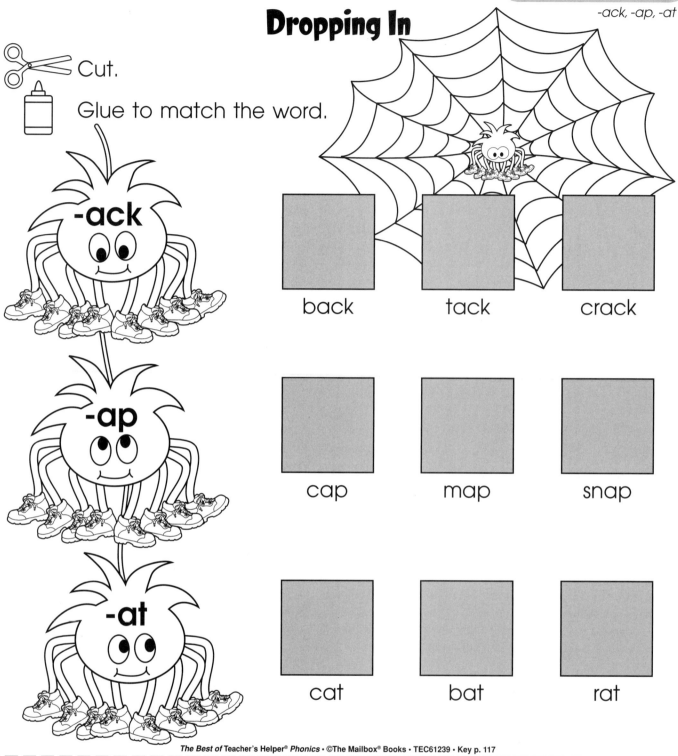

-ack

back	tack	crack

-ap

cap	map	snap

-at

cat	bat	rat

Name ______________________

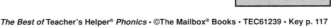

Web Words

Write **-ell** or **-est** to complete each word.

Cut. Glue to match each word.

-ell
-est

b ___ ___ ___

sh ___ ___ ___

y ___ ___ ___

n ___ ___ ___

v ___ ___ ___

ch ___ ___ ___

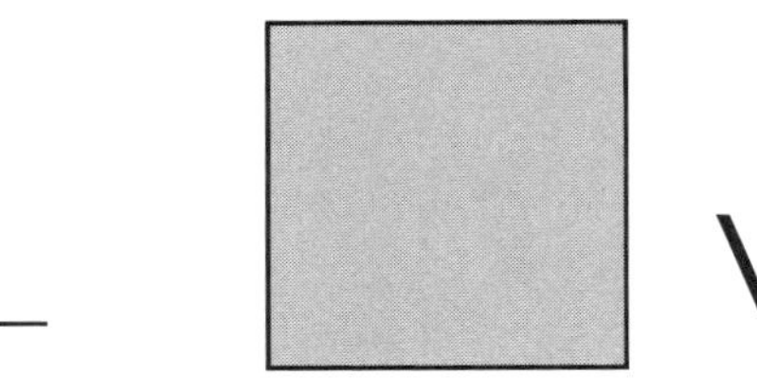

Pumpkin Climber

Write **-in, -ip,** or **-it** to complete each word.

Cut. Glue to match each word.

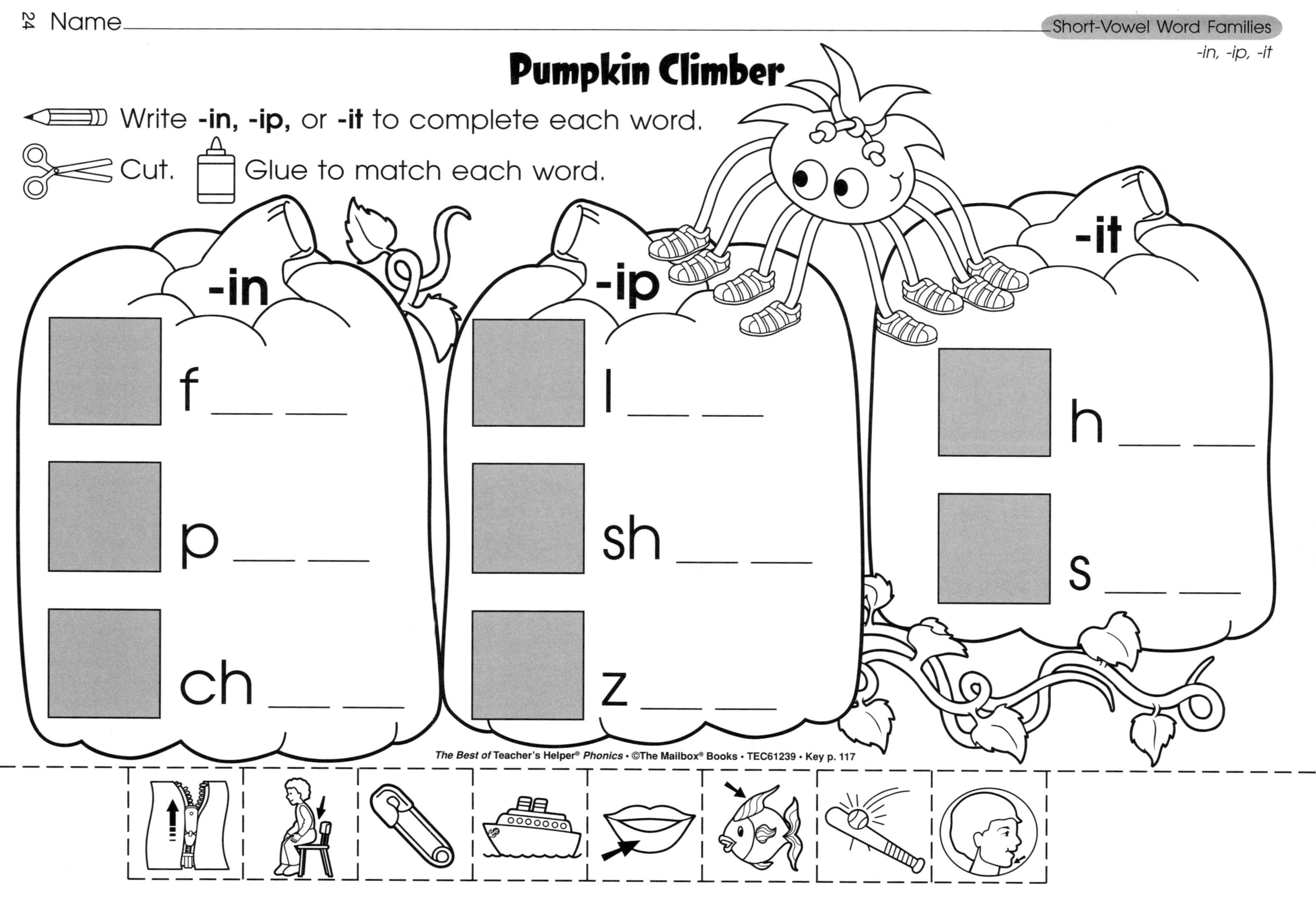
-in
f ___ ___
p ___ ___
ch ___ ___
-ip
l ___ ___
sh ___ ___
z ___ ___
-it
h ___ ___
s ___ ___

The Best of Teacher's Helper® *Phonics* • ©The Mailbox® Books • TEC61239 • Key p. 117

Name ____________________

Spider Friends

Write **-ock** or **-op** to complete each word.

Cut. Glue to match each word.

STOP
-ock
bl ___ ___ ___
s ___ ___ ___
cl ___ ___ ___
r ___ ___ ___
-op
m ___ ___
st ___ ___
t ___ ___
h ___ ___

Name ____________________

Fall Feet

Write the word for each picture.

 -uck			
 -ug			
 -ump			

Name________________________________

Early Birds

Cut. Glue to match the word families.

Write the word for each picture.

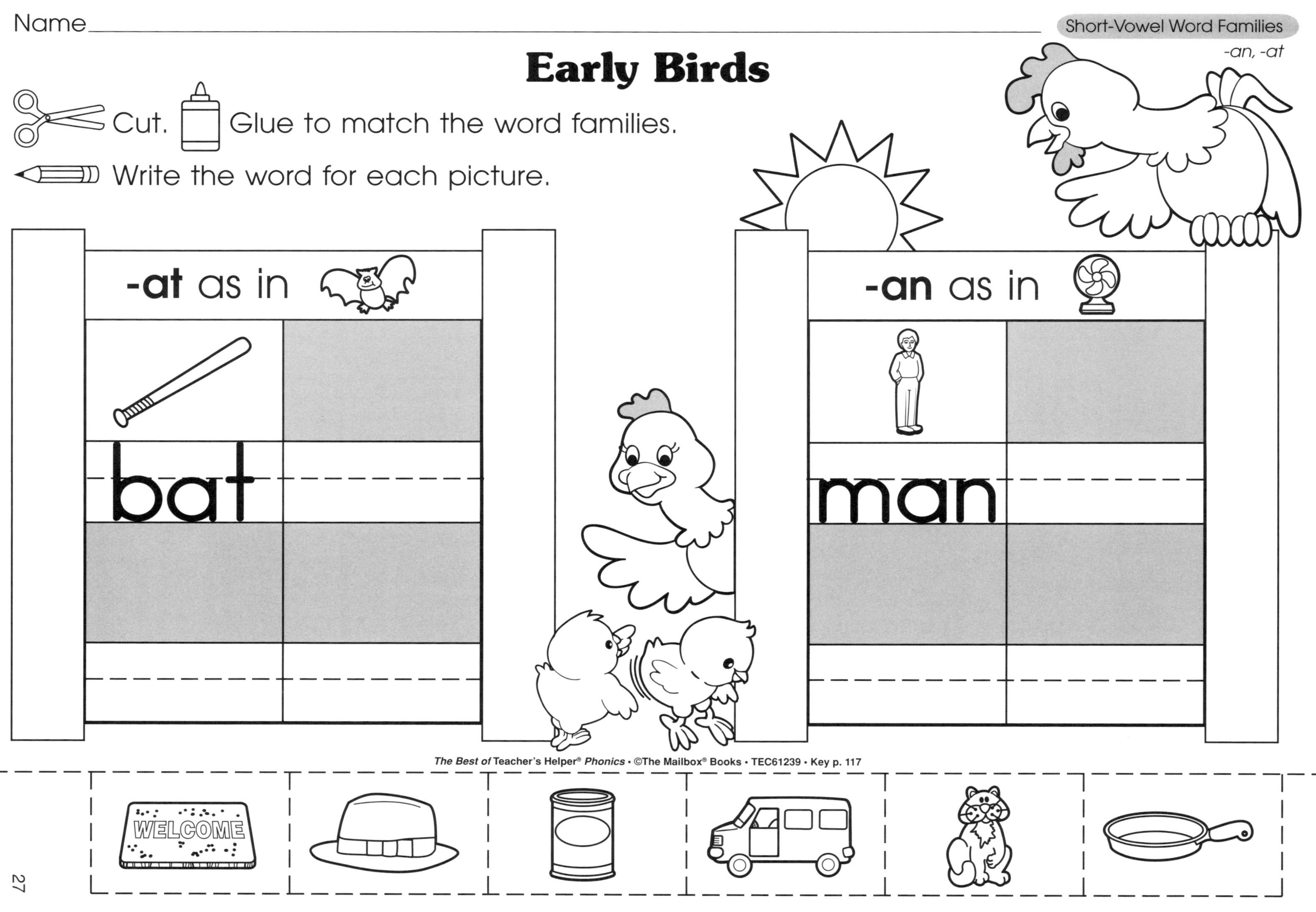
-at as in
bat
-an as in
man
WELCOME

Name ____________________

Family Meal

Cut. Glue to match the word families.

Write the word for each picture.

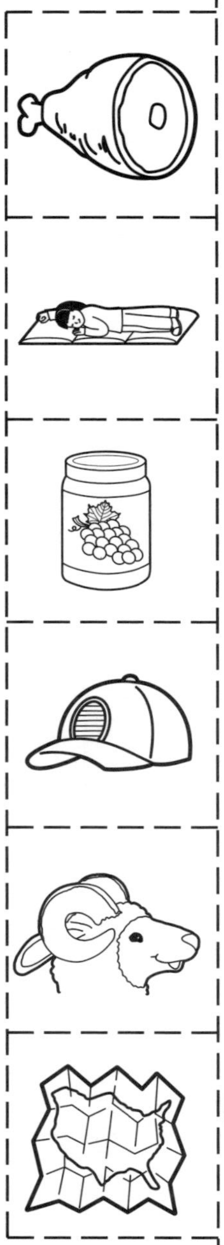

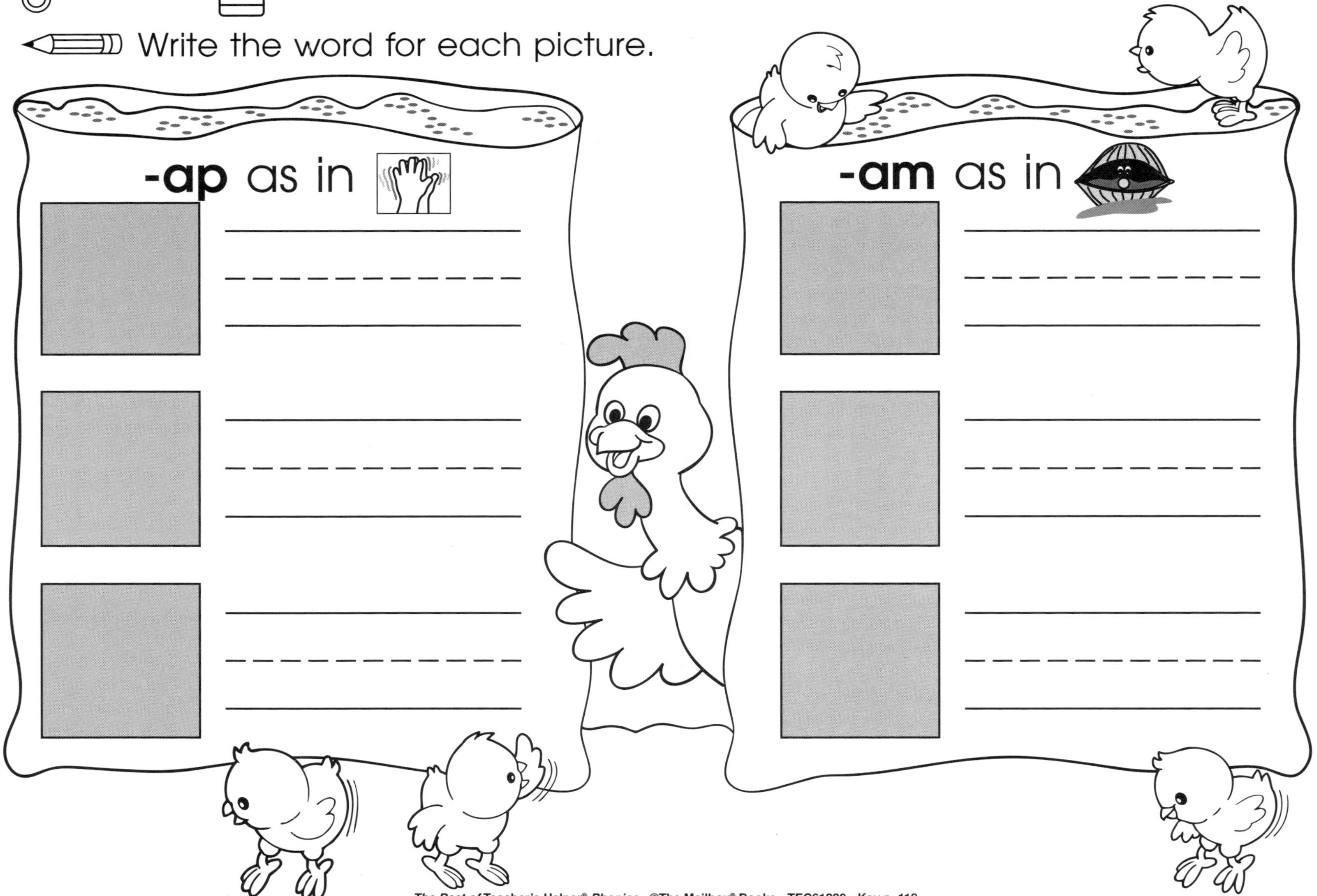

-ap as in

______

-am as in

______

Name________________________________

Henhouse

Read.

Color by the code.

Write each word below its matching word family.

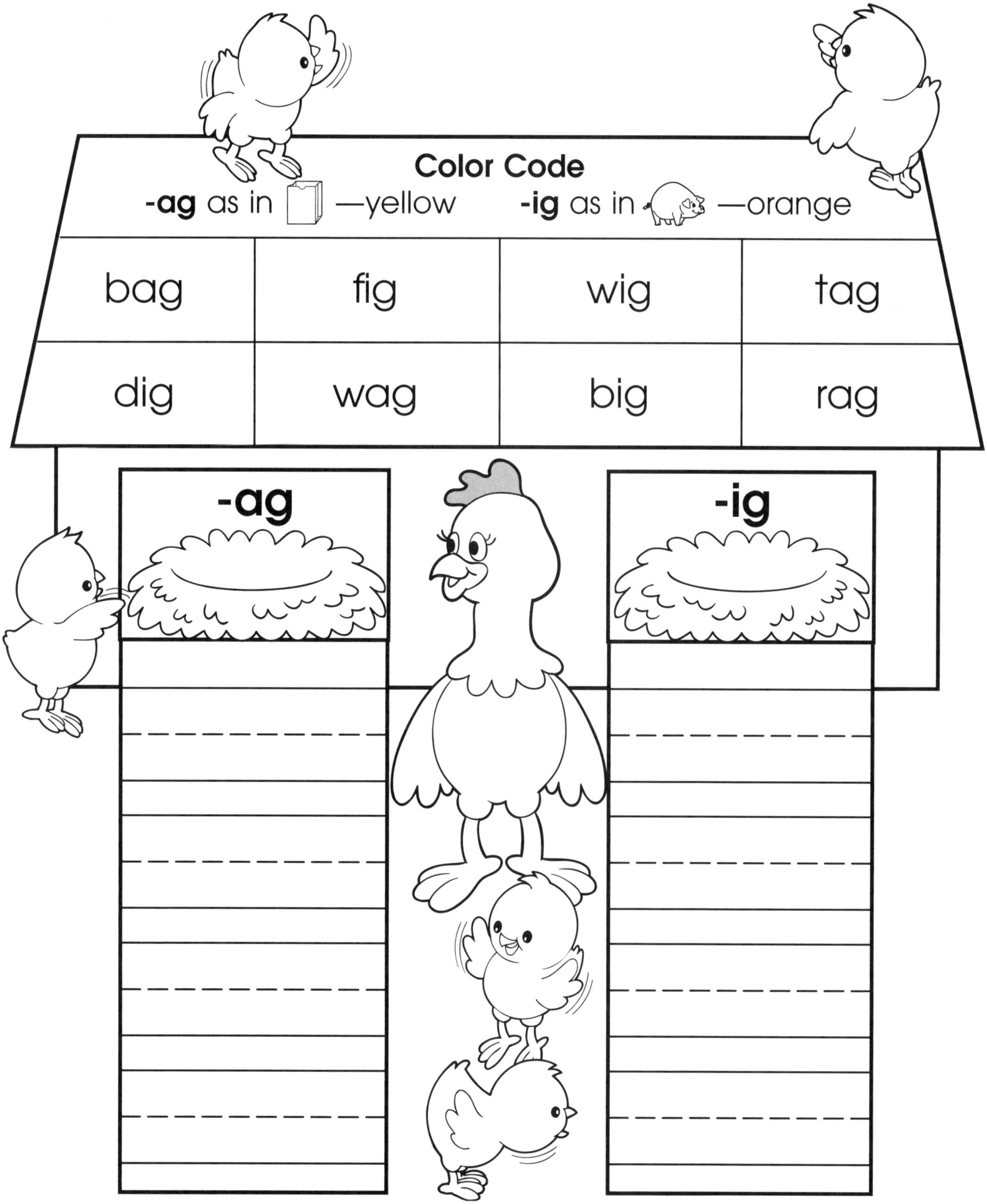

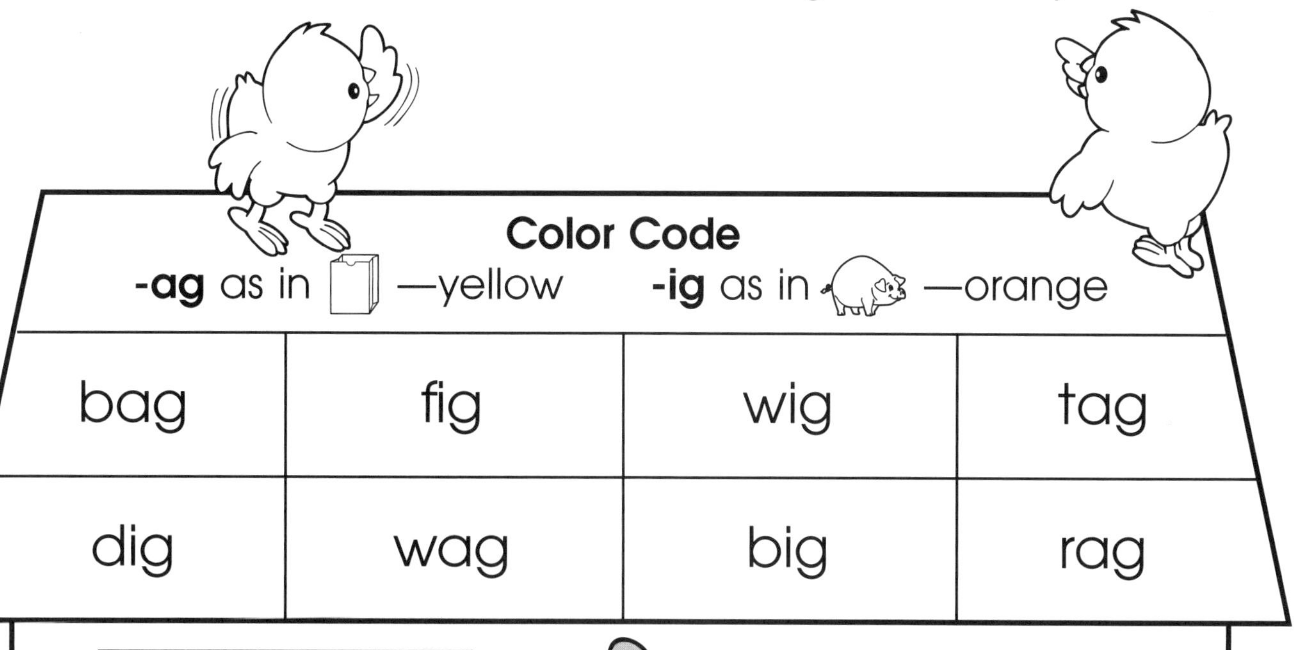
Color Code
-ag as in —yellow
-ig as in —orange
bag
fig
wig
tag
dig
wag
big
rag

-ag	-ig

Name____

Stacks of Hay

Read.

Color by the code.

Color Code

-ack as in — red

-ock as in — orange

-uck as in — yellow

duck	pack	dock
lock	sack	tack
puck	luck	rock

Write each word below its matching word family.

-ack	-ock	-uck

Name ____________________

Learning to Fly

Read.

Color by the code.

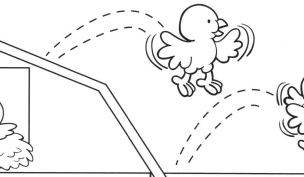

Color Code

-all as in (baseball) — yellow

-ill as in (grill) — red

will | call

fall | bill

hill | tall

Complete each sentence with a word that is on a barn door.

1. I have a one-dollar ____________.
2. Did you see the man ____________?
3. Please ____________ me later.
4. How ____________ are you?
5. The chick is on the ____________.
6. How ____________ you get home?

Name________________________________ Short Vowels

Choosing Chocolates

a, e, i

Write **a, e,** or **i** to complete each word.
Color a matching candy.

i
e
a
i
e
e
i
a
a
i

1. c ____ t

2. h ____ n

3. b ____ b

4. y ____ t

5. r ____ n

6. c ____ n

7. r ____ b

8. sh ____ p

9. j ____ t

10. k ____ ck

Name ____________________

Space Race

Cut. Glue to match the vowel sounds.

Write.

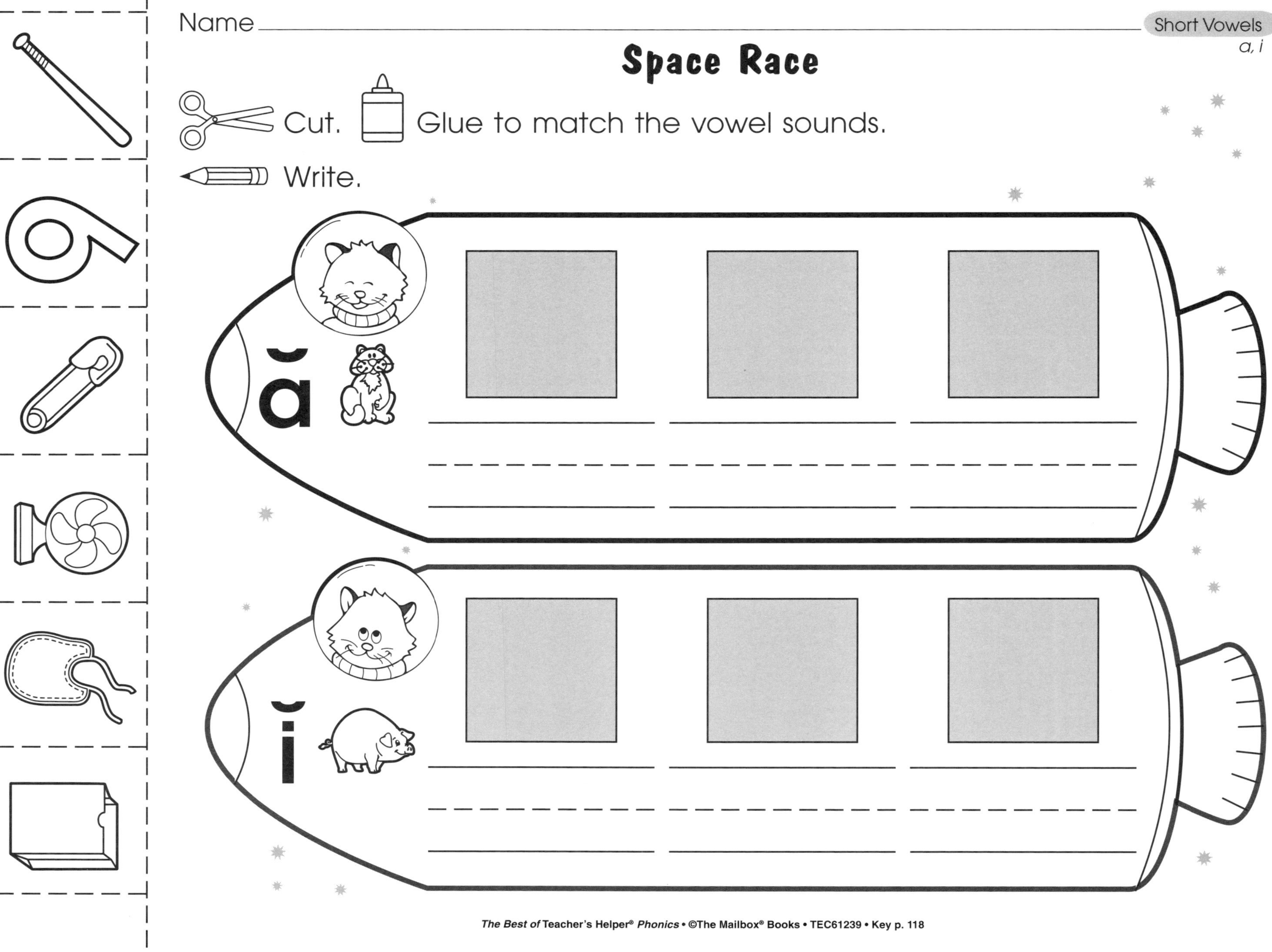
ă
ĭ

Name ____________________

Shoot for the Stars!

Color each big star by the code.

Write each word below the correct vowel.

Color Code

ă as in  —orange

ŏ as in  —yellow

ă

ŏ

Bonus Box: Pick one **ă** word and one **ŏ** word. Write sentences with them on the back of this paper.

Name________________________________

Zero Gravity

Circle the best word for each sentence.

Write.

1. We can ______________ in the sand.
   dog dig rag

2. Stop at the ______________ of the hill.
   pin tap top

3. Did you see my black ______________ ?
   hot hat him

4. The frog will ______________ to the pond.
   hop hip map

5. Is the fan in the ______________ box?
   bag big fog

6. Is the small ______________ hot?
   pit pop pan

Bonus Box: On the back of this paper, write a sentence with each of these words:
tap **tip** **top**

Name ______________________

Cool Craters

Color each circle by the code.

Write.

Color Code

ĕ as in (bell) —red

ŭ as in (bus) —blue

1. ______

2. ______

3. ______

4. ______

5. ______

6. ______

7. ______

8. ______

Bonus Box: Look at the words you wrote for numbers 1 and 2. Use each word in a sentence on the back of this paper.

Name ____________________ Short Vowels *e, u*

Countdown Cats

Circle the best word for each sentence.

Write.

1. He just got off the ____________.
   bet bus best

2. Is your ____________ in the sink?
   lot beg mug

3. Put the eggs in the ____________.
   nut nest not

4. The ____________ can swim well.
   desk duck dot

5. I set the ____________ on the desk.
   pen push pond

6. Will you ____________ this for me?
   cot cut met

7. Can we ____________ your dog?
   put pot pet

Name ____________________

Satellite Fix

Cut.

Glue to match the vowel sounds.

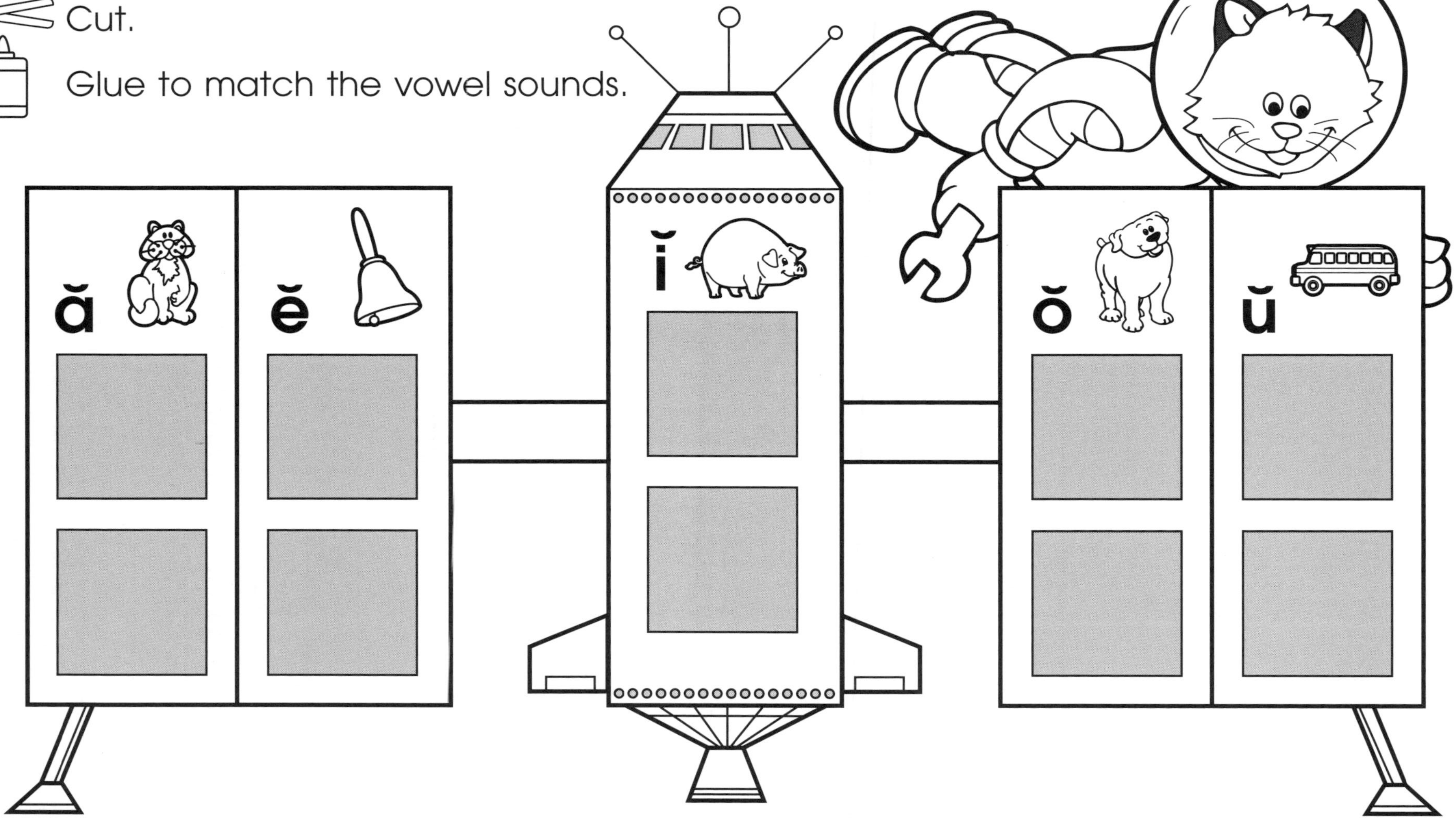

ă

ĕ

ĭ

ŏ

ŭ

Name________________________________

In Flight

Write the short **e** word that matches each clue.
The first one has been done for you.

1. a word for chicken 
h e n

2. write with this 

3. a number word 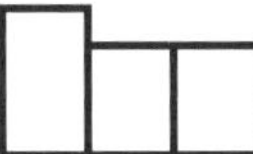

4. more than one man 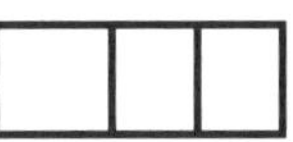

5. a home for a bear 

6. sleep outside in this 

7. not straight 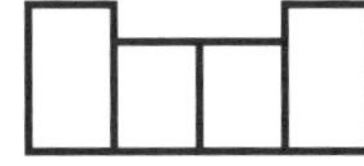

8. a word for a penny 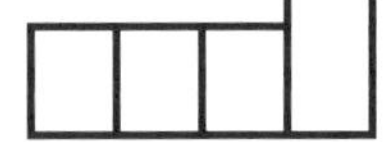

Name________________________________

Take a Peek!

Cut.
Glue each picture in the row with the matching word family.
Write each word.

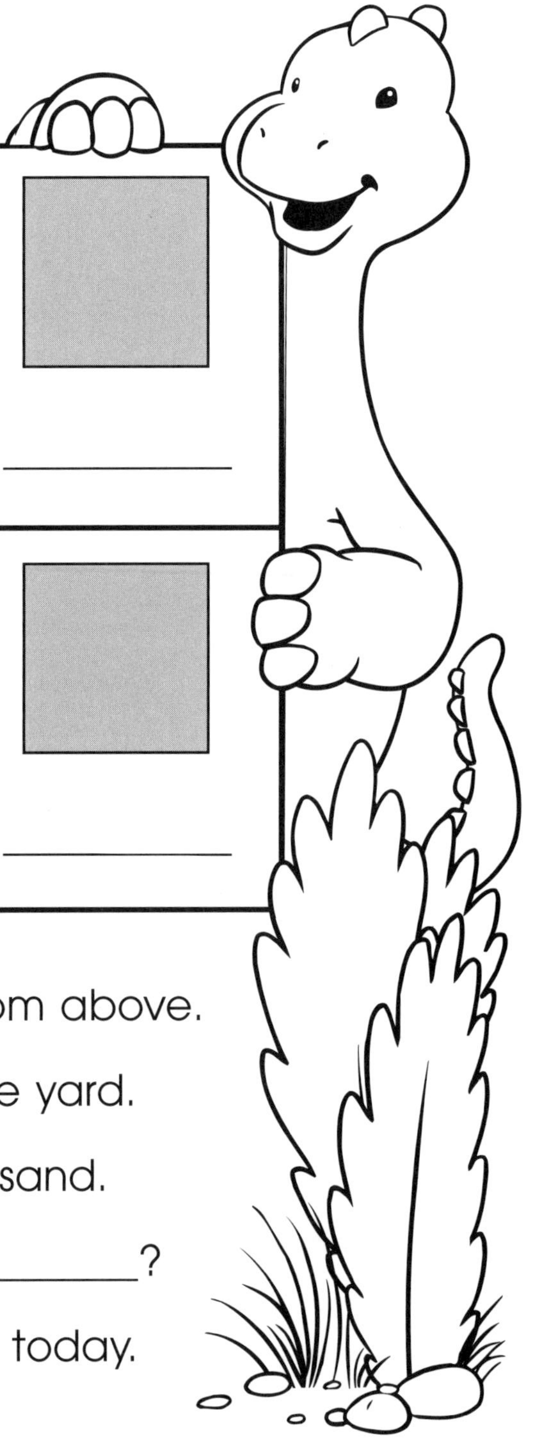

-ail	________	________	________
-ake	________	________	________

Complete each sentence with a word from above.

1. He will ______________ the leaves in the yard.
2. The ______________ is full of rocks and sand.
3. Would you like some birthday ______________?
4. I hope that I get some ______________ today.

Name ____________________

Look Who's Here!

Cut.
Glue below the matching word family.

-ain
-ate

Complete each sentence with a word from above.

1. I think it will ______________ later today.
2. Please close the garden ______________.
3. The ______________ will leave at two o'clock.
4. He can't be ______________ for school.
5. Put my lunch on a paper ______________.

Bonus Box: Choose a word from each group. Write a sentence with each word on the back of this sheet.

pain	date	gate	rain
late	chain	train	plate

Name ____________________

A Leafy Lunch

Cut. Glue each picture below the matching word family.
Write each word.

-ice

-ight

50¢

Complete each sentence with a word from above.

1. The __________ have long tails.
2. Shake the two __________.
3. When do you go to bed at __________?
4. Please turn on the __________.
5. Read the __________ tag.

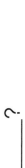

Name ____________________

Simply Huge!

Cut. Glue below the matching word family.

-ide
-ight

Complete each sentence with a word from above.

1. Now it's my turn to go down the ______________.
2. The sun is very ______________ this morning.
3. He said to go ______________ and drive for one mile.
4. My dad's new desk is big and ______________.
5. Where is the best place to ______________ this gift?

wide	right	hide	light
tight	bride	bright	slide

Name ____________________

A Giant List

Complete each sentence with a word from the word bank.
Color each matching footprint.
(Two words will not be used.)

1. I can't wait for the ______________ to stop!
2. Roll the ______________ to play the game.
3. That is too ______________ to fit in the box.
4. She will ______________ a card for her mom.
5. When my dog sees me, it wags its ______________.
6. She cooked white ______________ for lunch.
7. Turn on the ______________ so that I can see.
8. You need to ______________ the bottle first.

Word Bank
shake
tail
pail
rice
dice
night
light
wide
make
rain

Bonus Box: Look at the word bank. Find the words that you did not use. Use them in sentences on the back of this paper.

Name____

In the Garden

Color by the code.

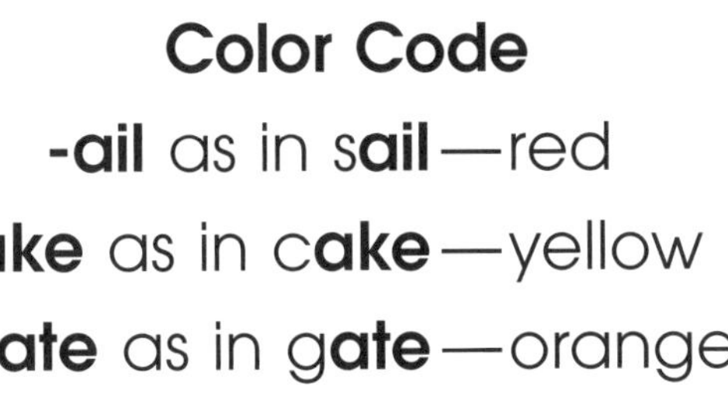
Color Code
-ail as in s**ail**—red
-ake as in c**ake**—yellow
-ate as in g**ate**—orange

pail
late
date
lake
bake
tail

Complete each sentence with a word from above.

1. What is the ____________ today?
2. Is it too ____________ to plant flowers?
3. Fill up the ____________ with dirt.
4. I will get water from the ____________.
5. Your ____________ is very long.
6. Now I will go and ____________ a pie.

Name____

Lots of Pots

Cut.
Glue to match.

mail	train	gate
plate	snail	rain

Complete each sentence with a word from above.

1. The ____________ crawls very slowly.
2. Is it going to ____________ today?
3. I hear a ____________ driving by.
4. I got a letter in the ____________.
5. Please shut the ____________.
6. Put the food on your ____________.

Name ______________________________

Taking a Rest

Cut.
Glue to match the word family.

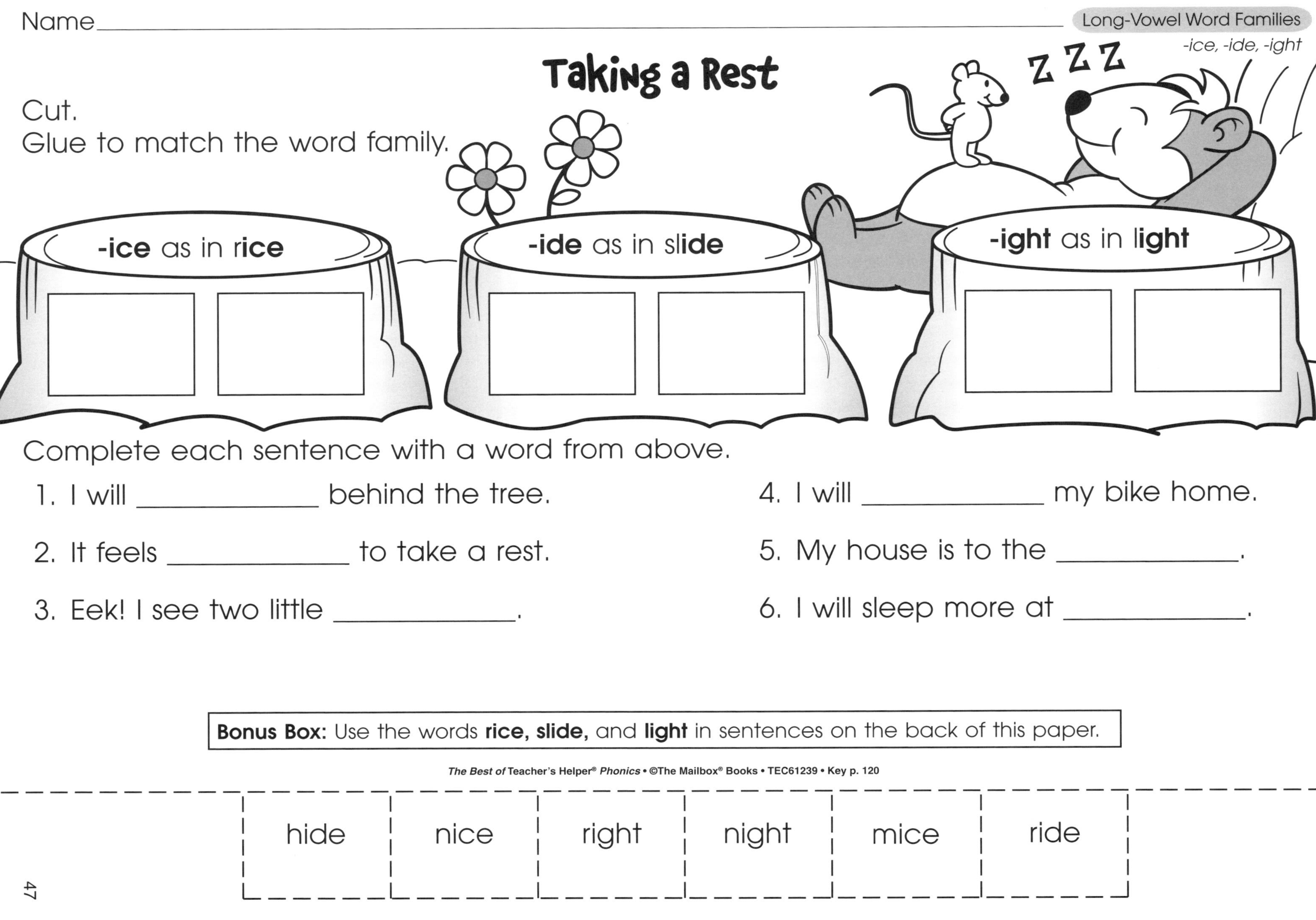
Z Z Z
-ice as in rice
-ide as in slide
-ight as in light

Complete each sentence with a word from above.

1. I will ____________ behind the tree.
2. It feels ____________ to take a rest.
3. Eek! I see two little ____________.
4. I will ____________ my bike home.
5. My house is to the ____________.
6. I will sleep more at ____________.

Bonus Box: Use the words **rice, slide,** and **light** in sentences on the back of this paper.

hide	nice	right	night	mice	ride

Name ______________________________

Growing Up!

Circle the word family in each word.
Write each word on a matching flowerpot.

Word Bank		
mine	bright	line
might	bride	slide

-ide
as in
r**ide**
-ight
as in
l**ight**
-ine
as in
f**ine**

Complete each sentence with a word from above.

1. The sun is very ____________ today.
2. Please wait your turn in the ____________.
3. These flowers are for the ____________.
4. Let's go play on the ____________.
5. I ____________ plant more flowers.
6. That big flower is ____________.

Name____

Starting Over

Write the word for each picture.
Use the word bank.

Word Bank

night	plate	dice	snake
nail	train	nine	slide

____________	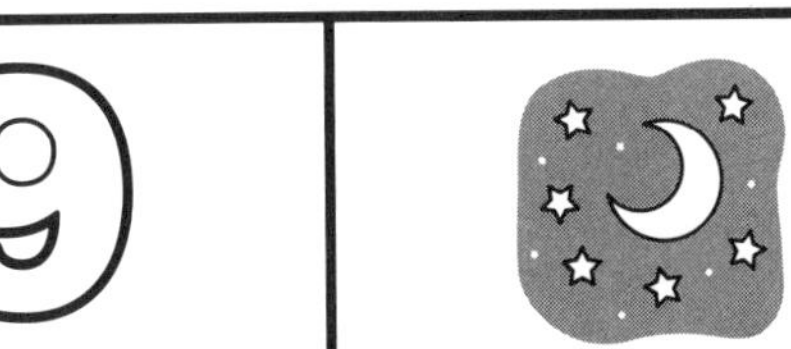 ____________	____________	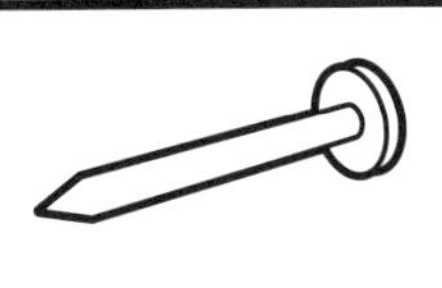 ____________
____________	____________	 ____________	 ____________

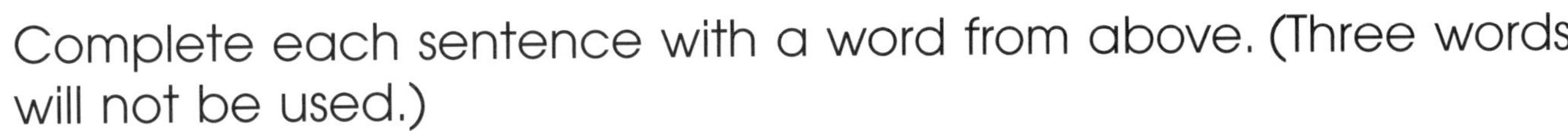

Complete each sentence with a word from above. (Three words will not be used.)

1. Bats like to fly in the dark at ____________.
2. It is your turn to roll the ____________.
3. I hear the ____________ coming down the track.
4. Use the hammer to put the ____________ in the wall.
5. It is fun to go down the ____________.

Name________________

Sandy Castles

Write.
Color by the code.
Use the word bank to help you.

Color Code
ea—yellow
ee—red

Word Bank

beak	sheep	queen	beach
dream	deer	east	wheel

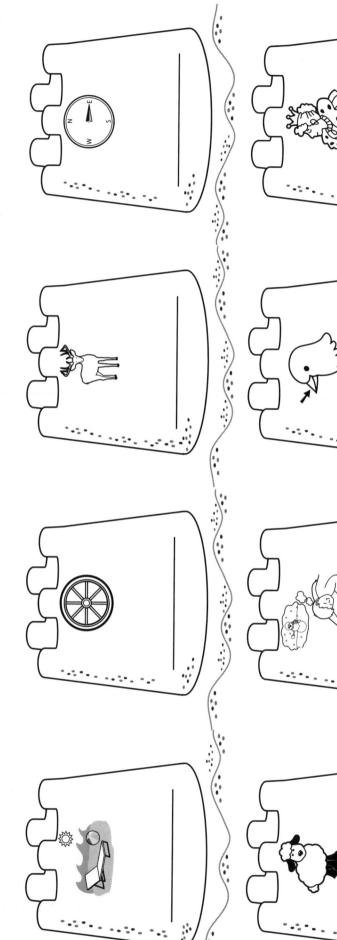

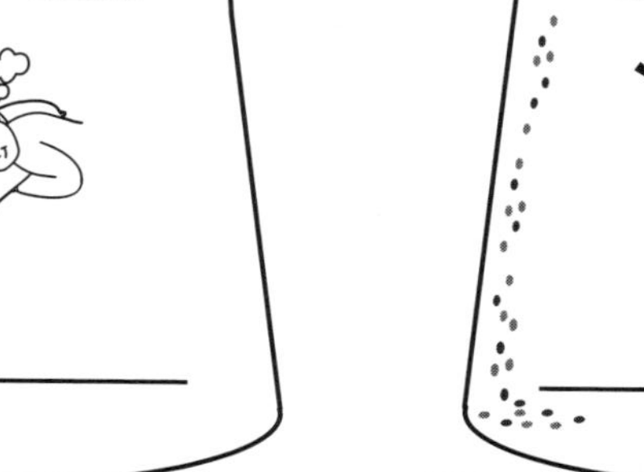

Name___________________________________

Rows of Roses

Write.
Use the word bank.
Color by the code.

Color Code

o_e as in **bone**
—orange

oa as in **boat**
—yellow

Word Bank

soap	goat	coat	road
cone	hose	note	rope

Bonus Box: On the back of this page, write two sentences that each have at least one word with the long *o* sound.

Name ____________________

One More Tune

Cut. Glue to match the vowel sounds.

ā		
ō		
ē		
ī		

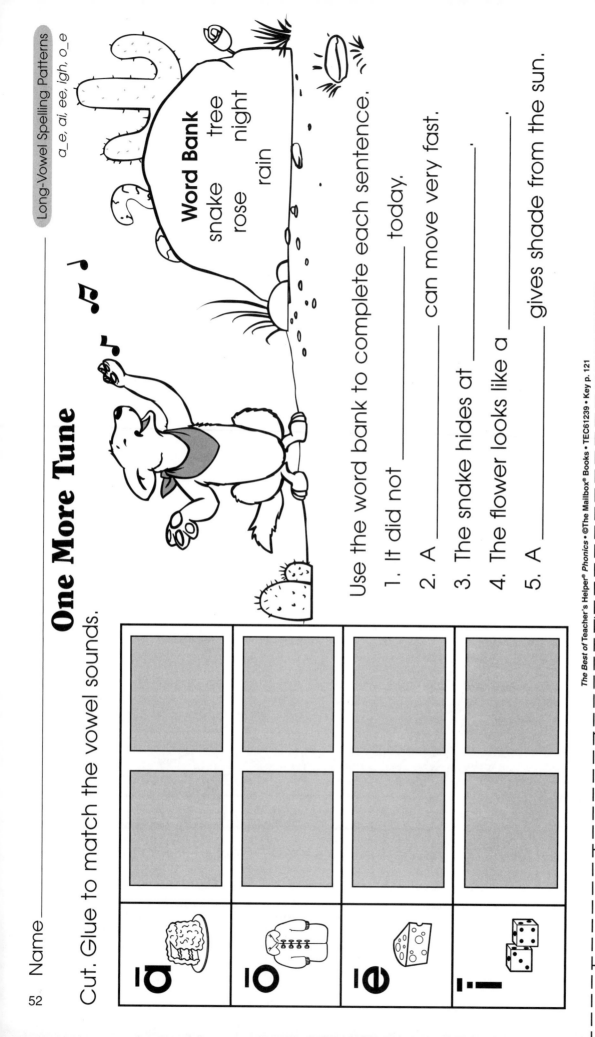

Word Bank
snake tree
rose night
rain

Use the word bank to complete each sentence.

1. It did not ____________ today.
2. A ____________ can move very fast.
3. The snake hides at ____________.
4. The flower looks like a ____________.
5. A ____________ gives shade from the sun.

9

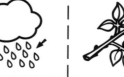

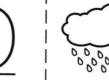

Name______________________________

Tricky Seals

Cut.
Glue to match.

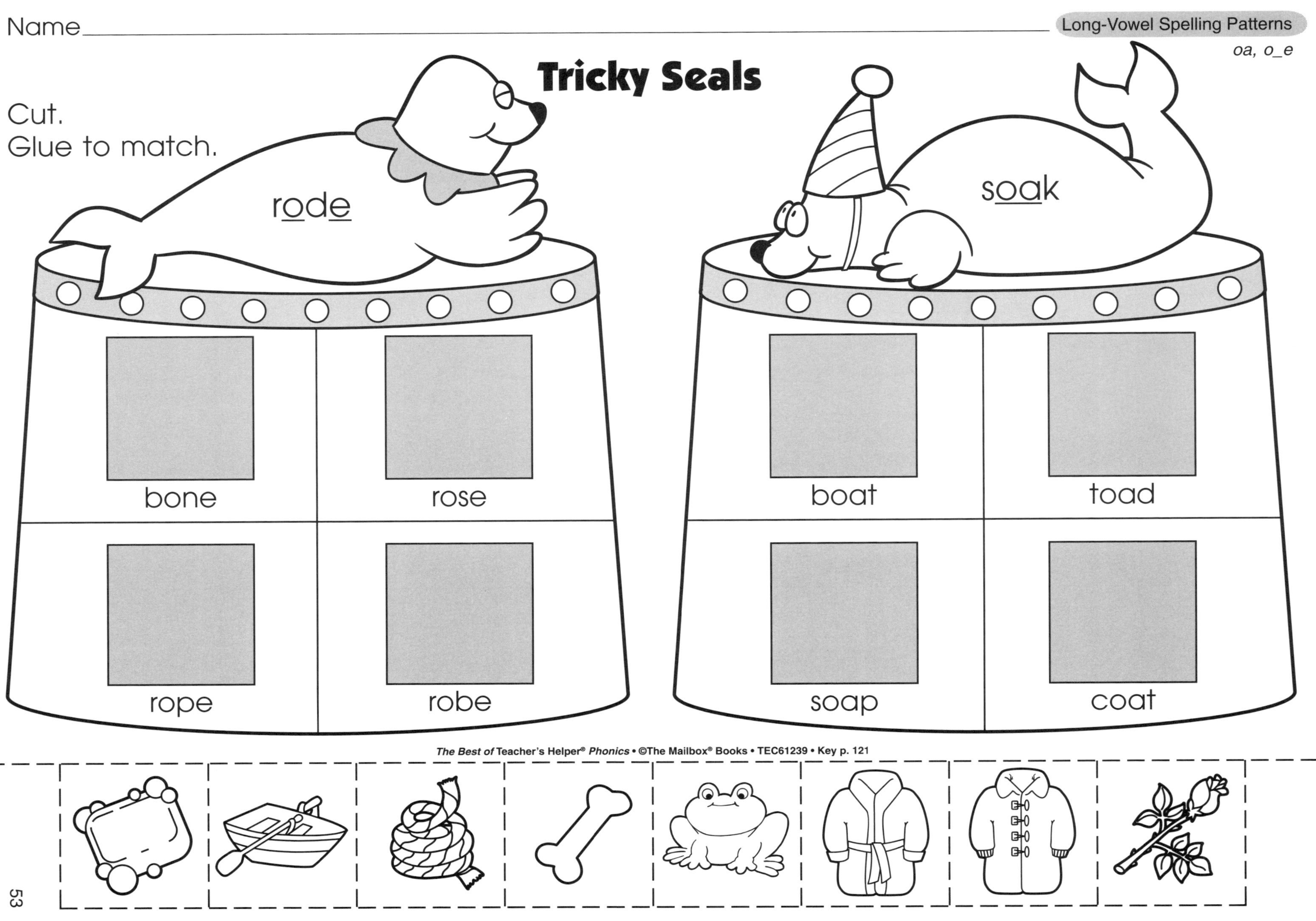
rode
soak
bone
rose
boat
toad
rope
robe
soap
coat

Name____

What a Show!

Color by the code.

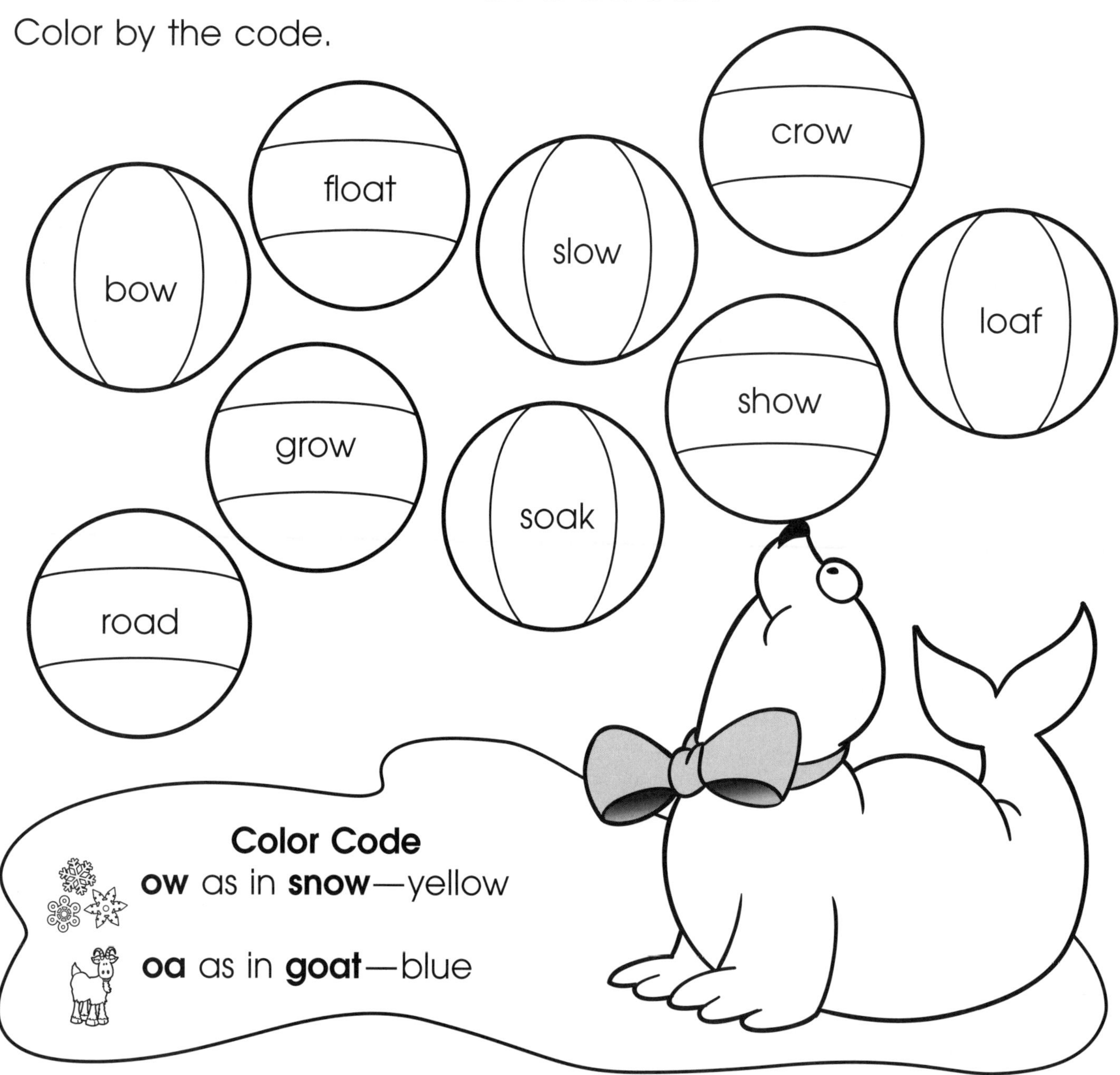
bow
float
slow
crow
loaf
grow
show
soak
road
Color Code
ow as in **snow**—yellow
oa as in **goat**—blue

Complete each sentence with a word from above.

1. Look at the cute ______________ on his neck.
2. Please get a mop and ______________ up the water.
3. I am glad I came to see this ______________!
4. The seal is fast, not ______________.
5. Can you ______________ in the water like a seal?

Name____

Making a Splash

Write.
Use the word bank.
Color by the code.

Word Bank
bead
feet
bee
three
beak
leaf
Color Code
ee as in deer—green
ea as in tea—blue
3

Name________________________________

A Team of Three

Word Bank

	deep	neat	see	
seal	feed	week	eat	beach

Complete each sentence with a word from the word bank.

1. These seals can do some ______________ tricks.
2. It's time to ______________ the hungry seals.
3. How many fish can a seal ______________?
4. The ______________ show will be starting soon.
5. They do five shows each ______________.
6. Did you ______________ them climb the stairs?
7. The water they swim in is very ______________.
8. I wonder whether seals like to live on the ______________.

Name____

Time for Treats

Read.
Color by the code.

Color Code
long o—blue
long e—green
note
seen
snow
teeth
road
goat
hole
meal
joke
clean
blow

Name____

Swimming School

Write the word for each picture.
Use the word bank.

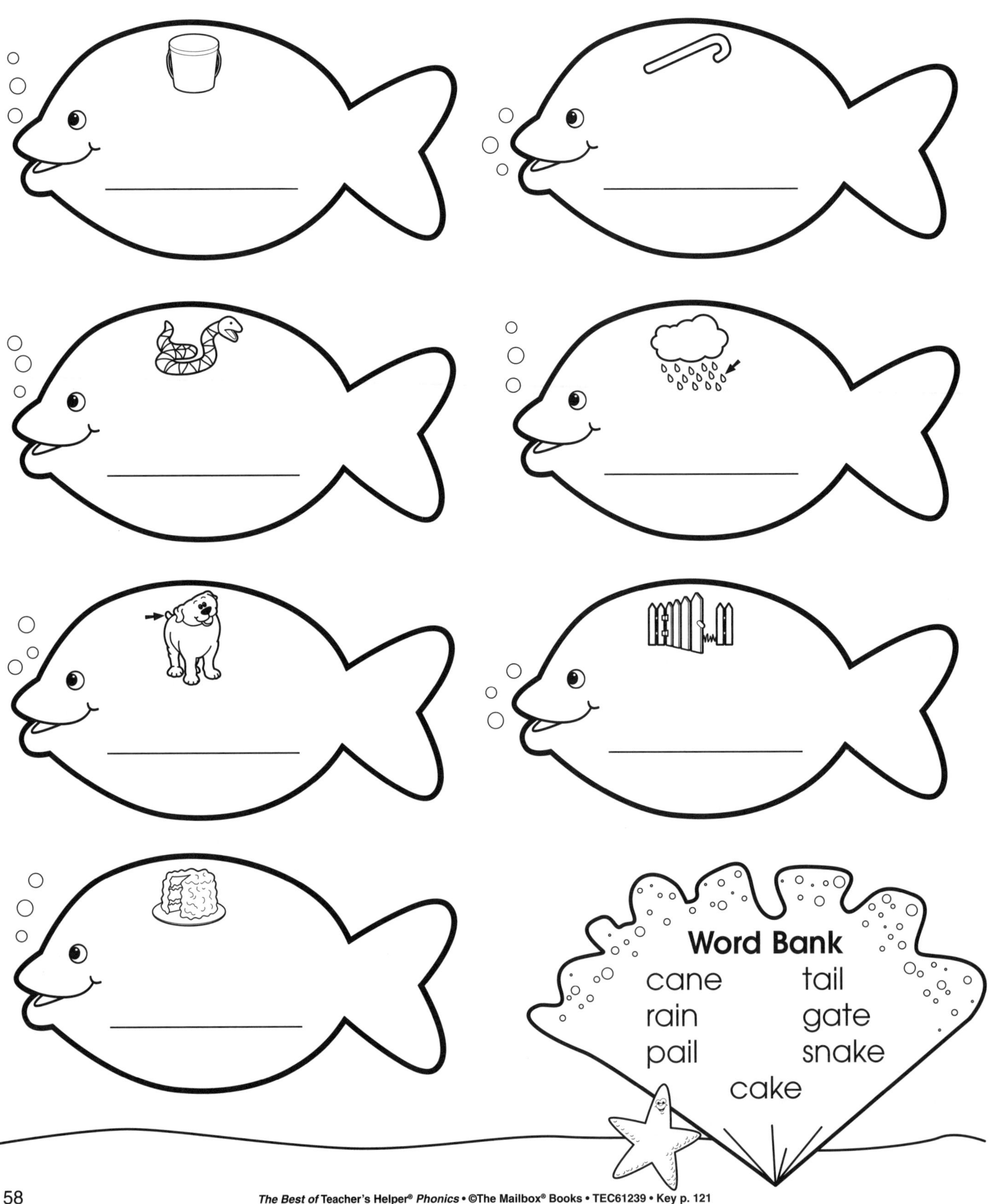
Word Bank
cane
tail
rain
gate
pail
snake
cake

Name ____

Play Day

Color by the code.

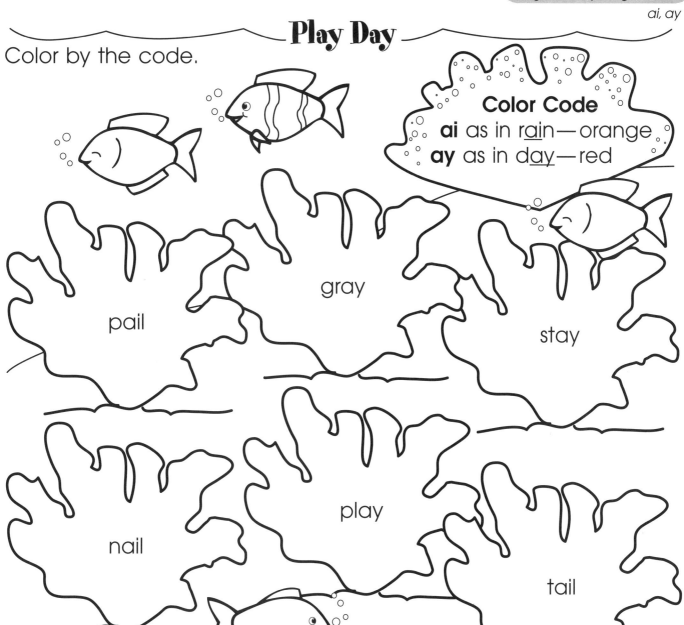

Color Code
ai as in r<u>ai</u>n—orange
ay as in d<u>ay</u>—red

gray

pail

stay

play

nail

tail

Complete each sentence with a word from above.

1. The fish has a long orange ____________.
2. Those fish like to ____________ games.
3. I see a ____________ of sand by the water.
4. Watch out for that sharp ____________.
5. Do you see the big ____________ whale over there?
6. Let's ____________ here and play today.

Name____ Long-Vowel Spelling Patterns

i_e, igh

Fish Food

Cut. Glue to match the vowel patterns.

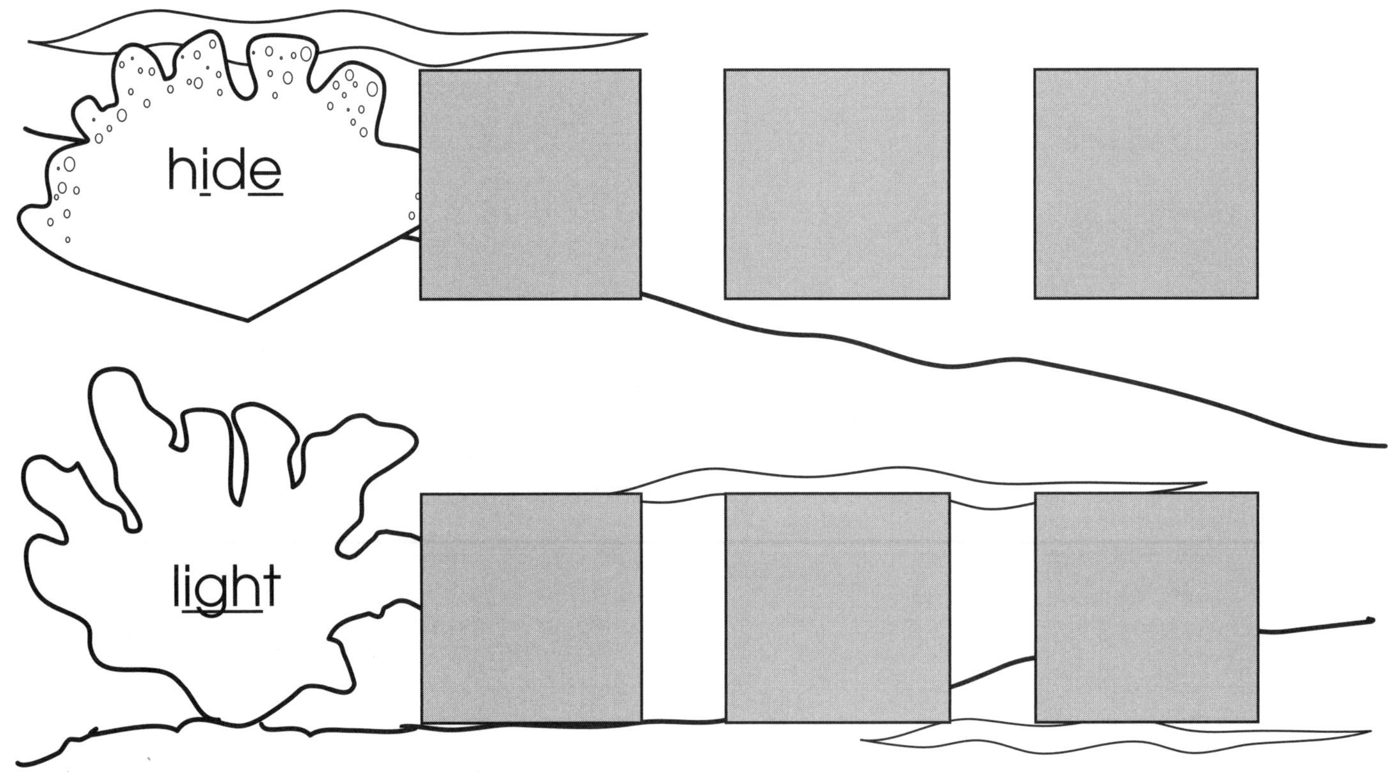

hide
light

Complete each sentence with a word from above.

1. There is a tasty green plant ____________ here.
2. It is very dark here at ____________.
3. Is it ____________ to eat dinner yet?
4. Do you ____________ to eat plants?
5. I will take a ____________ of this plant.
6. I can jump up ____________ above the water.

time	night	high	like	bite	right

Name ____

Under the Sea

Color by the code.

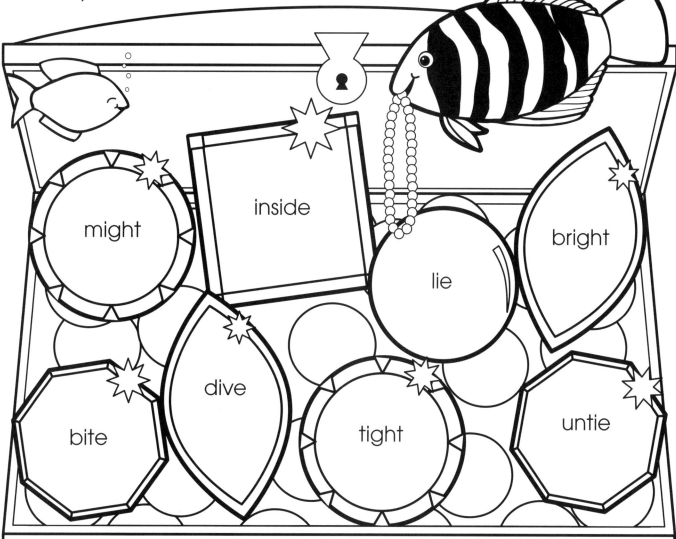

might

inside

bright

lie

dive

bite

tight

untie

Color Code

ie as in pie—red **igh** as in night—yellow **i_e** as in bike—blue

Complete each sentence with a word from above.

1. It is fun to swim and ____________.
2. That ____________ be a treasure!
3. I hope you are not telling a ____________.
4. What could be ____________?
5. Let's ____________ the rope and open it!
6. Look at all the ____________ colors!

Name____

Safe From the Rain

Write the word for each picture.
Use the word bank.

Word Bank
cake snail
train chain
plane snake

Complete each sentence with a word from above.

1. The ________________ has a pretty orange shell.
2. Will they fly on the same ________________?
3. The ________________ keeps the gate closed.
4. There is a long green ________________ in the garden.
5. The ________________ went very fast on the tracks.
6. Who gave him the little birthday ________________?

Name ____

A Rainy Play Date

Read.
Color the raindrops by the code.

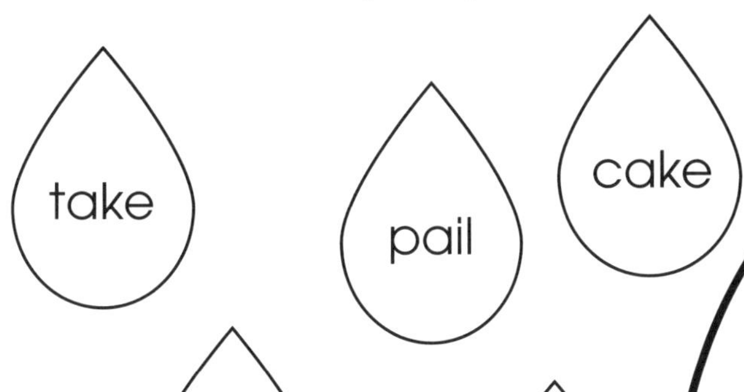

take | pail | cake | play | made | wait | mail | name | stay | may

Color Code
rain — blue
day — green
game — yellow

Complete each sentence with a word from above.

1. I got a letter in the ________________ today.
2. The letter ________________ me very happy.
3. Do you want to ________________ a game now?
4. You ________________ take the first turn.
5. We can ________________ for the rain to stop.
6. Can you help me bake a ________________ later?

Bonus Box: Choose a blue, green, and yellow raindrop from above. Use the words in sentences on the back of this paper.

Name________________________________

Wet Feet

Cut. Glue to match the vowels.
Read each group of words.

team	

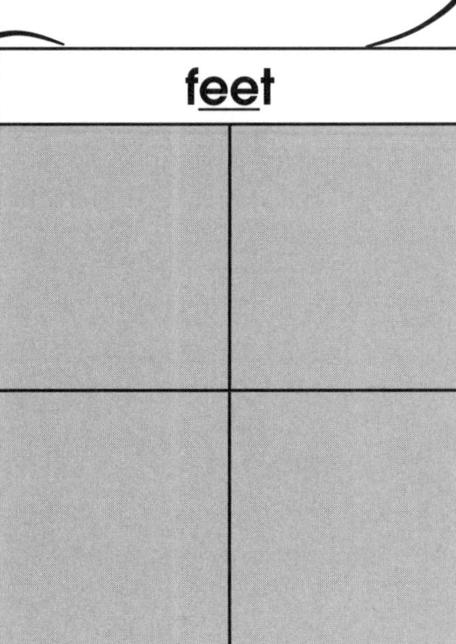

feet	

Complete each sentence with a word from above.

1. Do you ______________ better today?
2. I feel very well this ______________.
3. It is a ______________ to play in the rain.
4. I would like a cup of hot ______________.
5. We can eat some ______________ apples.
6. When are you going to the ______________?

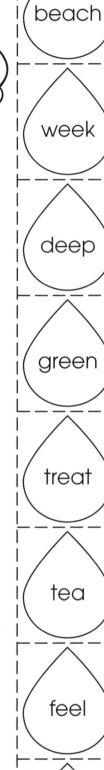

beach

week

deep

green

treat

tea

feel

leaf

Name ____________________

Duck Crossing

Circle the long *i* words.
Write each long *i* word on the matching umbrella.

1. There are many clouds up high.
2. Mom says that walking in a line is nice.
3. We always turn right at the light.
4. We are going about one more mile.
5. We might get there before night.
6. Maybe we can drive a red car next time.

dime
sight

Name____

What a Sight!

Circle the long *o* words.

1. Did I forget my coat at home?
2. The rain might soak me today.
3. I put a note beside the stove.
4. I hope we can ride in a boat on Monday.
5. It is always fun to float on the water.
6. I saw a little toad jump on a stone.

Write each long *o* word below the word with the matching vowels.

road	**bone**
______________	______________
______________	______________
______________	______________
______________	______________
______________	______________

Bonus Box: Use the words **road** and **bone** in sentences on the back of this paper.

Name________________________________

A Skating Pair

Cut. Glue to match vowel sounds.

ă
as in
ā
as in

Bonus Box: Choose one short-vowel word and one long-vowel word from above. On the back of this page, write each word in a sentence.

Name______________________________________

e

Ski Lift

 Cut.  Glue to match vowel sounds.

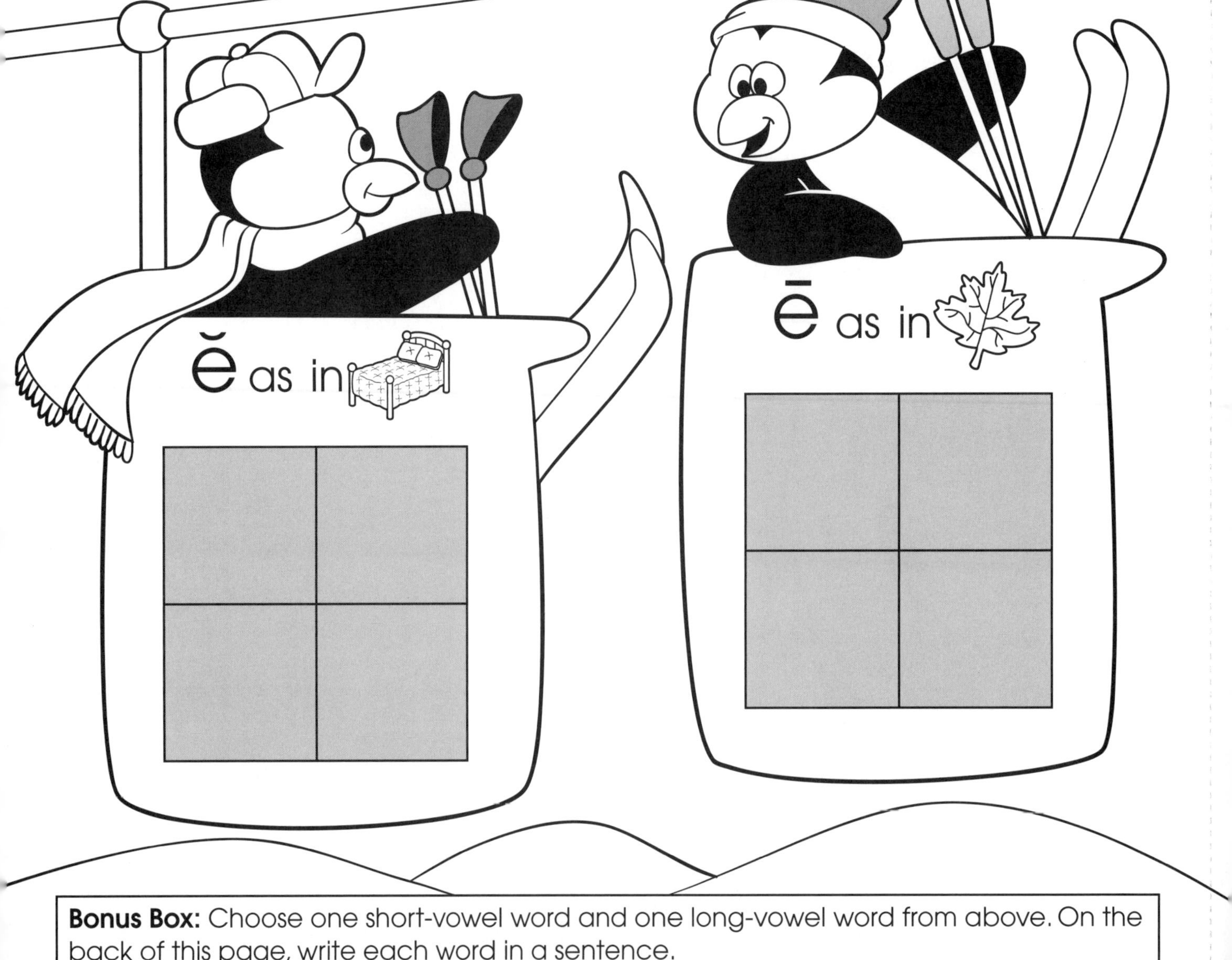

ĕ as in

ē as in

Bonus Box: Choose one short-vowel word and one long-vowel word from above. On the back of this page, write each word in a sentence.

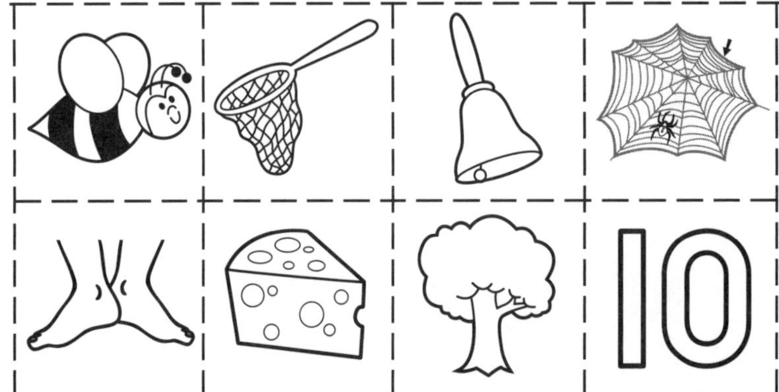
10

Name ______________________________

Lacing Up

Cut. Glue to match vowel sounds.

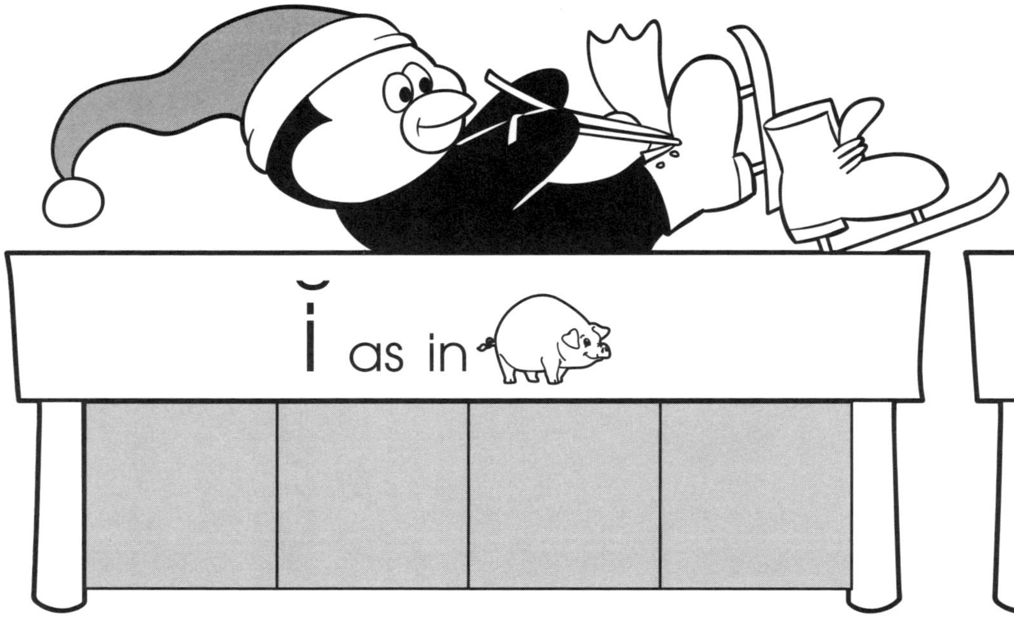

ĭ as in

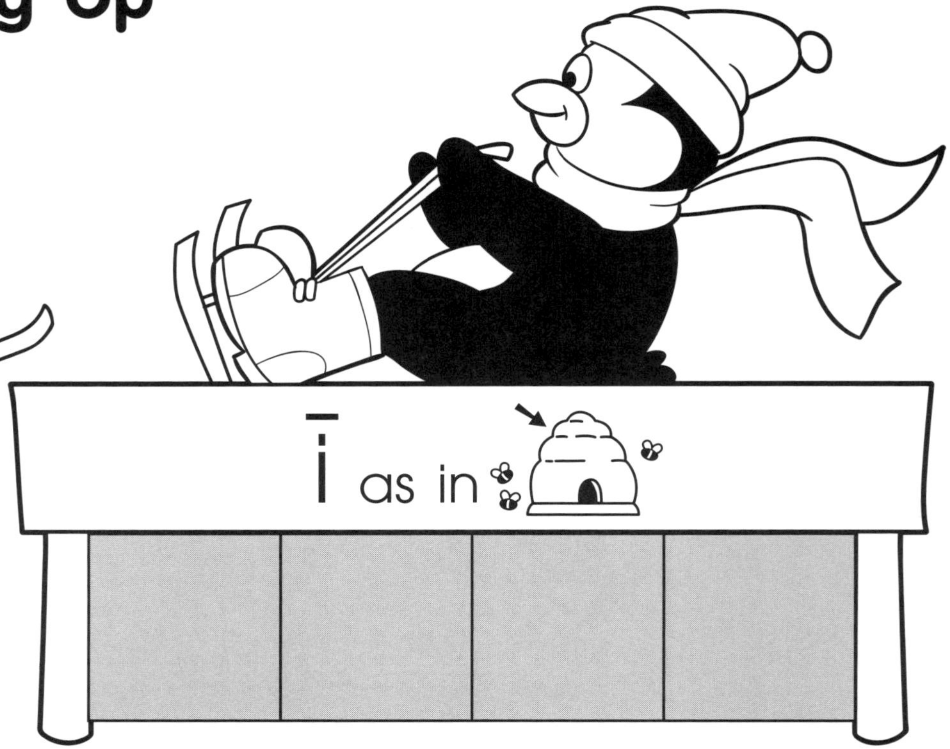

ī as in

5

LIBERTY
IN GOD WE TRUST

Bonus Box: Choose one short-vowel word and one long-vowel word from above. On the back of this page, write each word in a sentence.

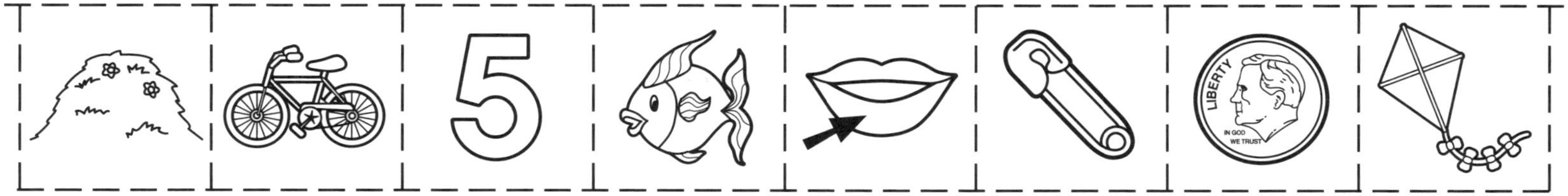

Name________________________________

Hit the Slopes

Cut. Glue to match vowel sounds.

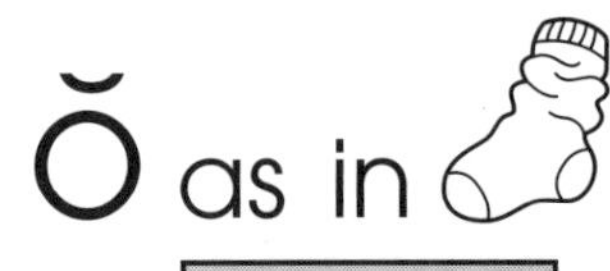
ŏ as in

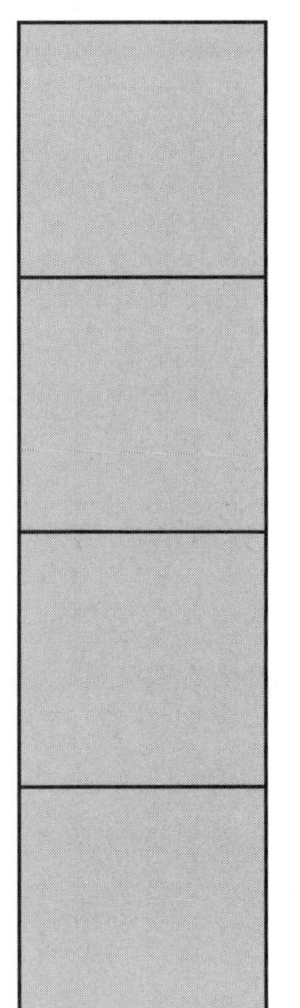

ō as in

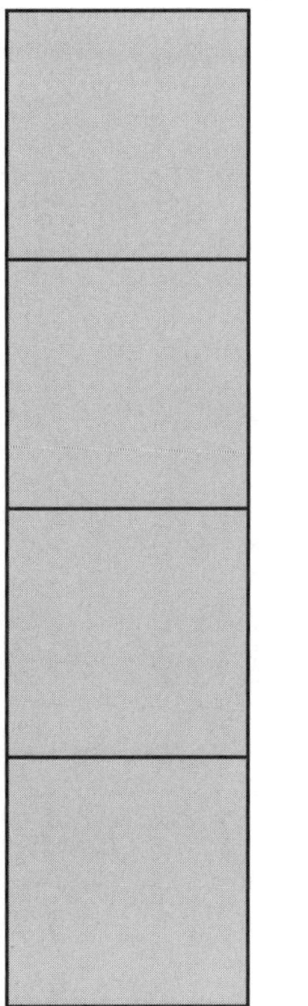

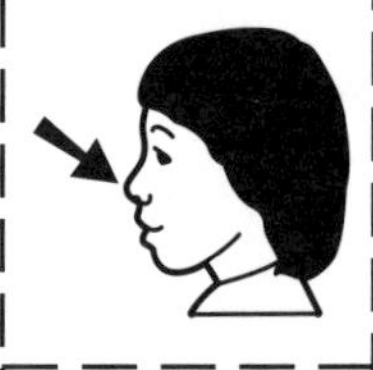

Bonus Box: Choose one short-vowel word and one long-vowel word from above. On the back of this page, write each word in a sentence.

Name ____________________

Coyote Tune-Up

Cut. Glue to match the vowel sounds.

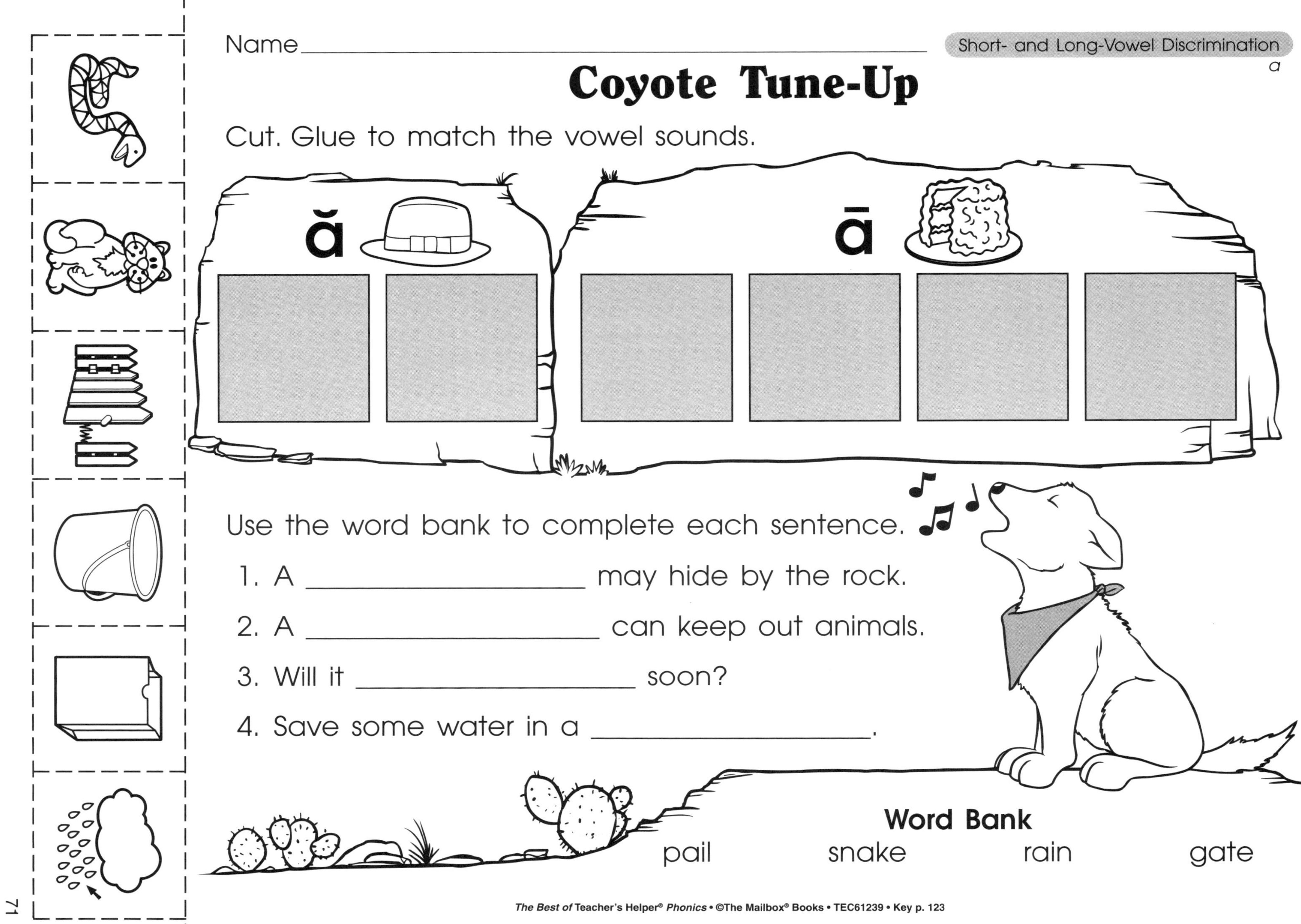
ă
ā

Use the word bank to complete each sentence.

1. A ________________ may hide by the rock.
2. A ________________ can keep out animals.
3. Will it ________________ soon?
4. Save some water in a ________________.

Word Bank

pail snake rain gate

Name____________________

Prickly Plants

Cut. Glue to match the vowel sounds.

ŏ
ō

Use the word bank to complete each sentence.

1. A ____________ smells nice.
2. We will go for a ride in a ____________.
3. Tie the ____________ to a rock.
4. A ____________ may eat the grass.

Word Bank
boat
rope
goat
rose

Bonus Box: On the back of this sheet, use the word **coat** in a sentence. Draw a picture to go with it.

11 12 1
10 2
9 3
8 4
7 6

Name________________________________

Sweet Dreams

Cut. Glue to match the vowel sounds.

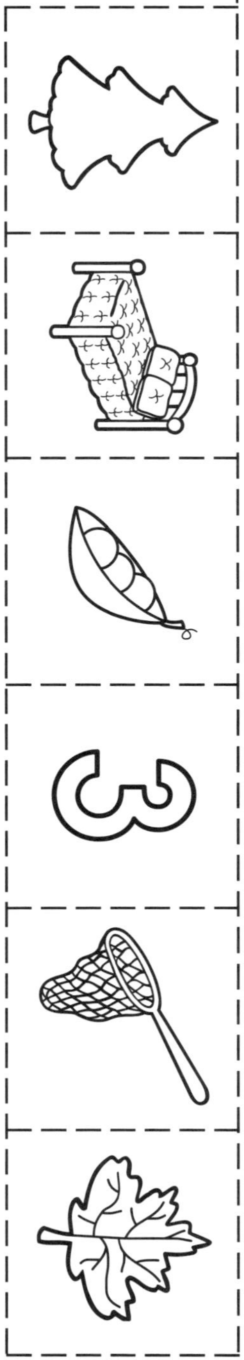

ĕ

10

ē

Use the word bank to complete each sentence.

1. He saw ____________ snakes.
2. A ____________ may fall off a tree.
3. Can ____________ grow here?
4. A bird sits in a ____________.

Word Bank

peas tree leaf three

Name________________________________

Sing a Song!

Cut. Glue to match the vowel sounds.

ĭ		

ī				

Use the word bank to complete each sentence.

1. It is a nice day to fly a ______________.
2. It gets cold at ______________.
3. The sun gives a lot of ______________.
4. He can sing ______________ songs.

Word Bank
night
five
kite
light

Bonus Box: On the back of this sheet, use the word **bright** in a sentence. Draw a picture to go with it.

Name ____________________

The Right Tools

Cut. Glue.
Write each word.
Use the word bank.

Word Bank

shell	cheese	thumb
chair	thorn	sheep
think	shovel	chip

ch 	____	____	____
sh 	____	____	____
th 13	 ____	 ____	 ____

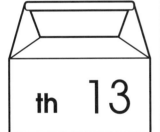

The Best of Teacher's Helper® *Phonics* • ©The Mailbox® Books • TEC61239 • Key p. 123

 Name ______________________

Whistle and Work

Cut. Glue.
Write each word.
Use the word bank.

Word Bank

shave	think
chin	wheel
thorn	chick
whale	shark

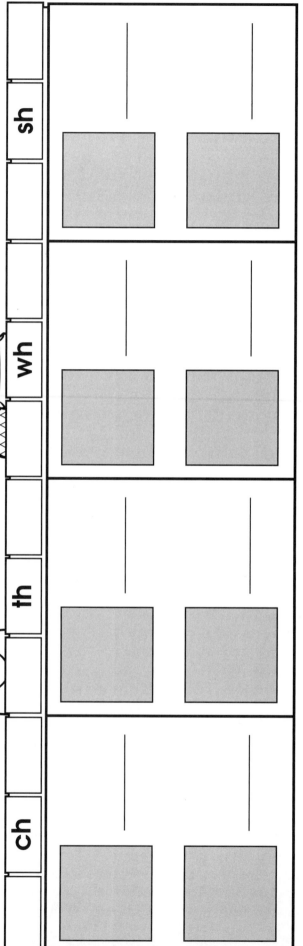

ch
th
wh
sh

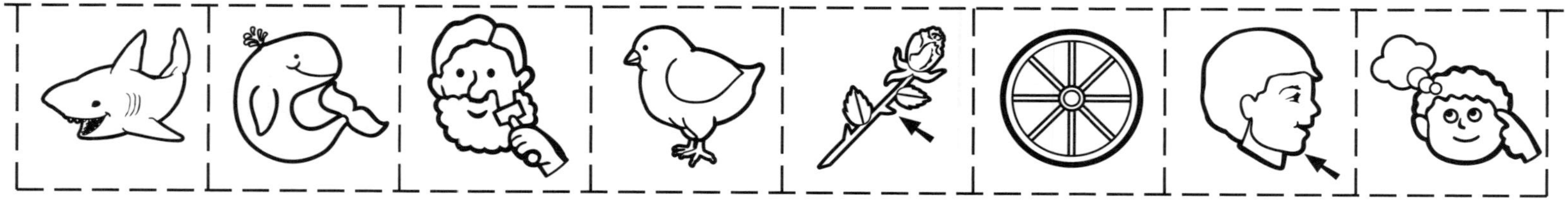

Name________________________________

At the Dock

Write **ch** or **sh.**
Color by the code.

__ __ick
__ __ark
__ __in
__ __ip
__ __air
__ __eep
__ __ovel
__ __ell
__ __ain
Color Code
sh as in — yellow
ch as in — red

Name ____________________

Fun on the Water

Write **ch, sh,** or **th.**

___ ___air
___ ___ink
___ ___ip
___ ___eck
___ ___irt
30
___ ___irty

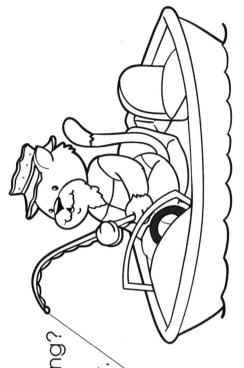

Use the words from above to complete the sentences.

1. Did you ________________ to see if we have everything?
2. Bring an extra ________________ in case you get wet.
3. I ________________ we are ready to go.
4. You can sit in the driver's ________________.
5. Watch out for the big ________________ on the lake!
6. I hope we catch ________________ fish!

Name______________________________

Happy House Painters

Write **ch** in each blank.

Cut. Glue.

____ in
____ eese
____ ain
____ air
____ ick
____ op
____ eek
____ erry

Name ________________________

Busy at the Barn

Write **sh** in each blank.

Cut. Glue.

____ ell
____ eep
____ ip
____ ave
____ ark
____ irt
____ oe
____ ovel

Name ____________________

A Bunch of Brushes

Write **ch, sh,** or **th** in each blank.
Read the paint colors.
Color each brush the matching color.

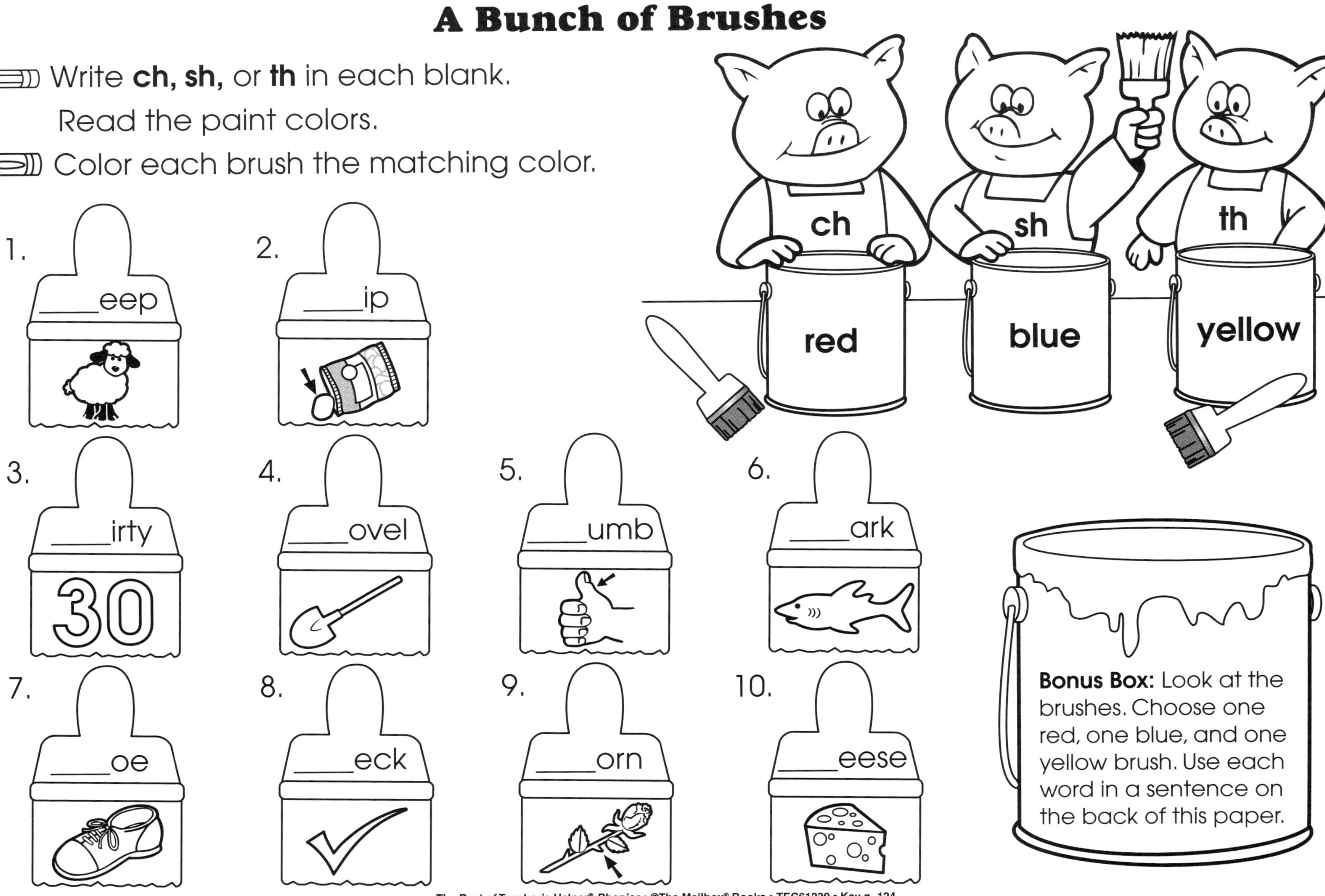
ch
red
sh
blue
th
yellow
1. ____eep
2. ____ip
3. ____irty
30
4. ____ovel
5. ____umb
6. ____ark
7. ____oe
8. ____eck
9. ____orn
10. ____eese
Bonus Box: Look at the brushes. Choose one red, one blue, and one yellow brush. Use each word in a sentence on the back of this paper.

Name________________________________ Consonant Digraphs *sh*

Great Teamwork!

Write each word below the correct picture.

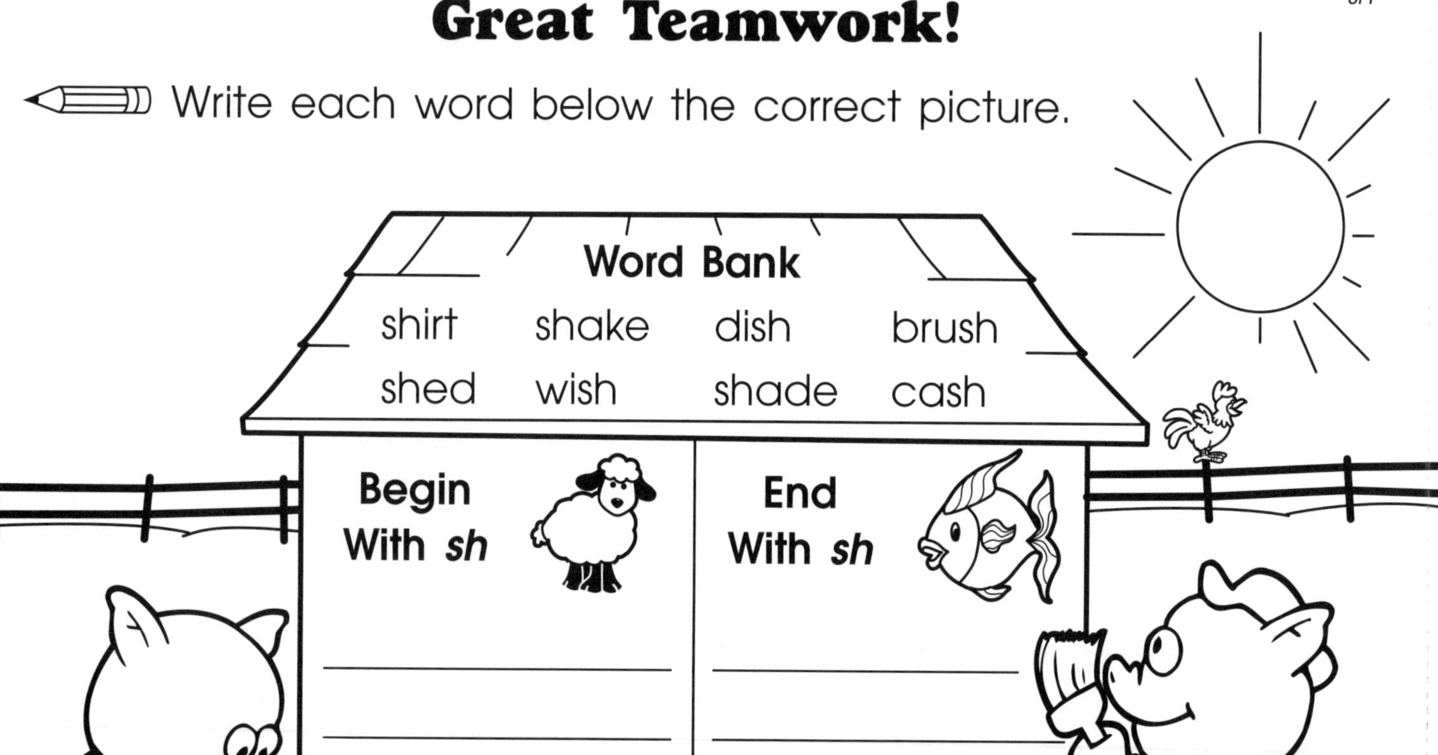
Word Bank
shirt
shake
dish
brush
shed
wish
shade
cash
Begin With *sh*
End With *sh*

Complete each sentence with the best word from above.

1. Did you ________________ that can of blue paint?
2. Dip your ____________________ into the green paint.
3. I ____________________ we had more things to paint.
4. I got some paint on my new ________________.
5. Put the paint cans in the old ________________.

Bonus Box: Use the words **dish** and **shade** in sentences on the back of this paper.

Name ____________________

Wet Paint

Write each word in the correct box.

Word Bank
with
thank
path
both
that
third
math
think

Begin With *th* 30	End With *th*
________ ________	________ ________
________ ________	________ ________

Complete each sentence with the best word from above.

1. That is the ____________ can of paint.
2. Do you ____________ we need more paint?
3. ____________ of us can go to the paint store.
4. What did you do ____________ the big brush?
5. ____________ you for helping me paint today.

Name________________________________

Jolly Jellyfish

Cut. Glue to match ending sounds.
Write each word.
Use the word bank.

Word Bank

beach	leash	brush
mouth	tooth	fish
	peach	wreath

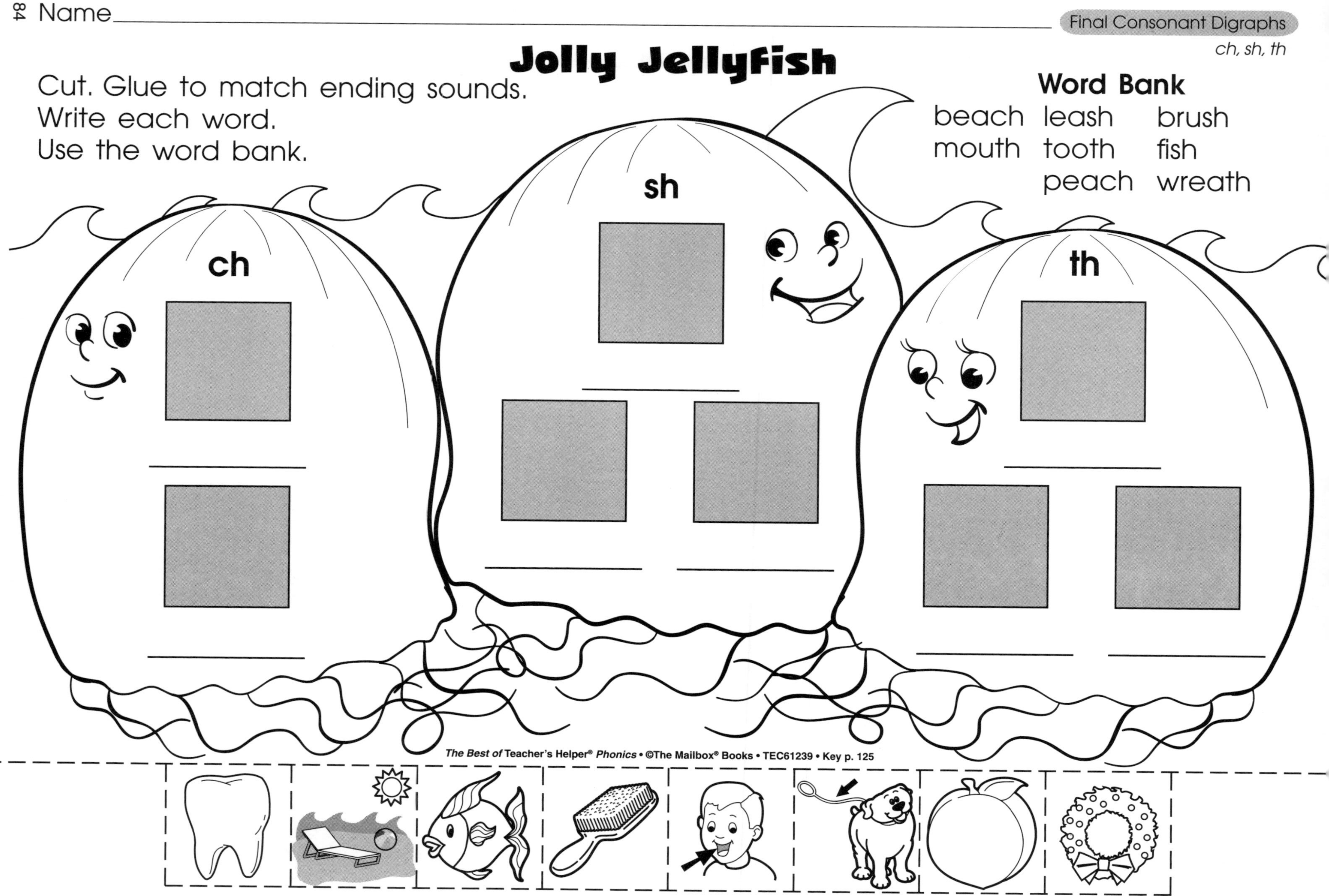
ch
sh
th

Name ________________________________

Taste Test

Cut. Glue to match the beginning sounds.

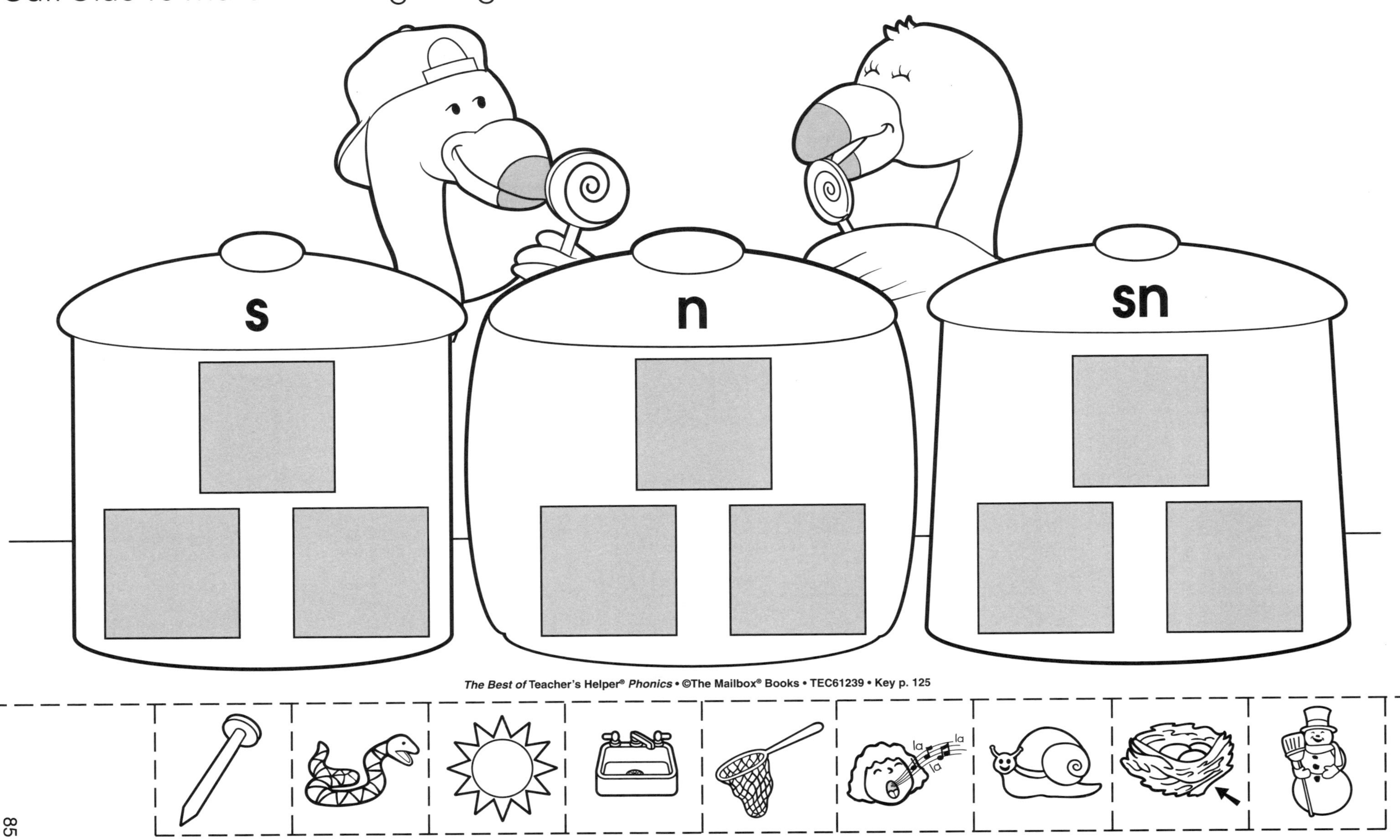
s
n
sn
la
la
la

Name____

Gumballs Galore

Color the gumballs by the code.

10
UNITED STATES
6
1¢
Color Code
st—orange
s—yellow
t—red

Name______________________________

Stop to Shop!

Complete each sentence with a word from the word bank.

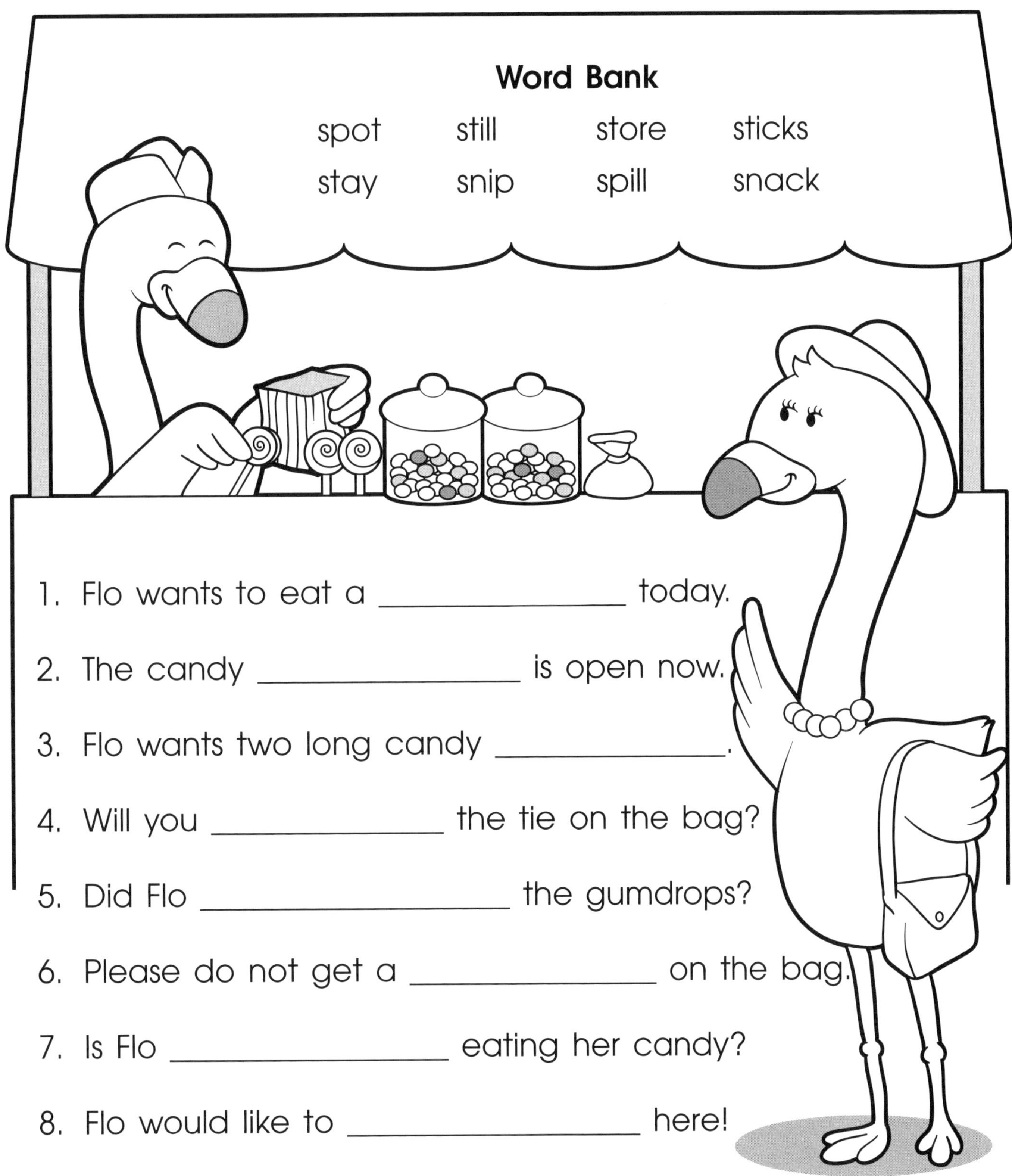

Word Bank

spot	still	store	sticks
stay	snip	spill	snack

1. Flo wants to eat a ______________ today.
2. The candy ______________ is open now.
3. Flo wants two long candy ______________.
4. Will you ______________ the tie on the bag?
5. Did Flo ______________ the gumdrops?
6. Please do not get a ______________ on the bag.
7. Is Flo ______________ eating her candy?
8. Flo would like to ______________ here!

Name ______________________________

Goodies to Go

Write **cl, fl,** or **pl.**

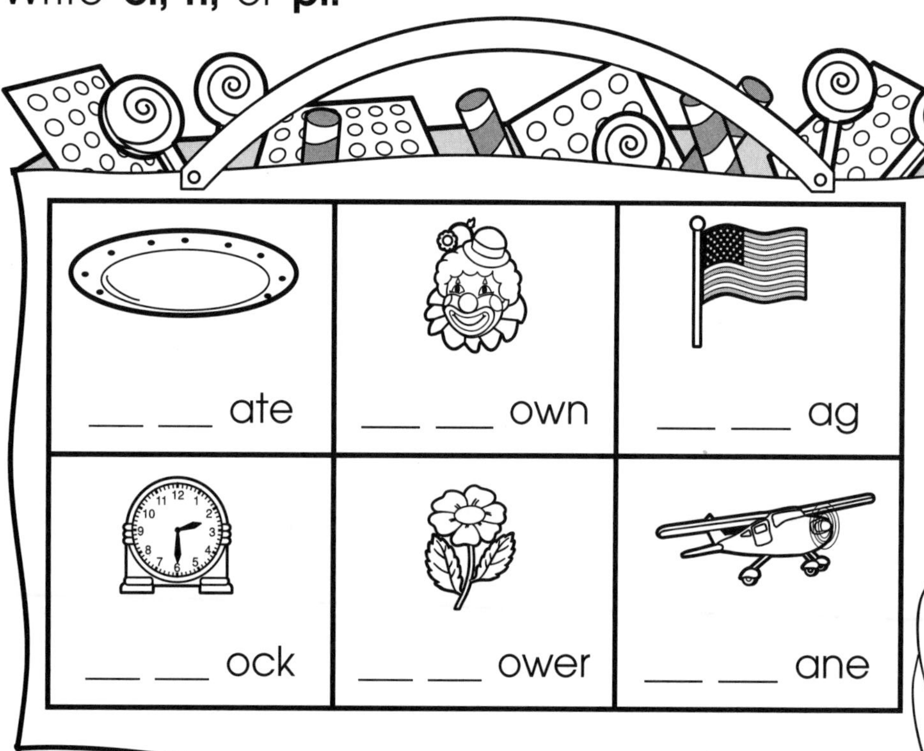
__ __ ate
__ __ own
__ __ ag
__ __ ock
__ __ ower
__ __ ane

Use the words above to complete the sentences.

1. The ______________ shows the time.
2. My ______________ is growing fast.
3. The ______________ has a silly hat.
4. Please put my cake on a ______________.
5. I will fly in a ______________ today.
6. He waves the ______________ in the air.

Sweet Treats

Bonus Box: On the back of this paper, use the words **clap** and **flap** in sentences.

Name________________________________

Fran's Famous Fudge

Write **br, fr,** or **gr.**

___ ___ apes
___ ___ ame
___ ___ oom
___ ___ uit
___ ___ ill
___ ___ ush
___ ___ og
___ ___ ead
I ❤ chocolate!

Use the words above to complete the sentences.

1. She will sweep with a big ____________________.
2. The ____________________ hopped into the water.
3. I picked seven green ____________________ today.
4. I made a sandwich with the ____________________.
5. Cooking on a ____________________ is a lot of fun.
6. I can fix my hair with the little ____________________.

Name________________________________

Candy Business

Complete each word.

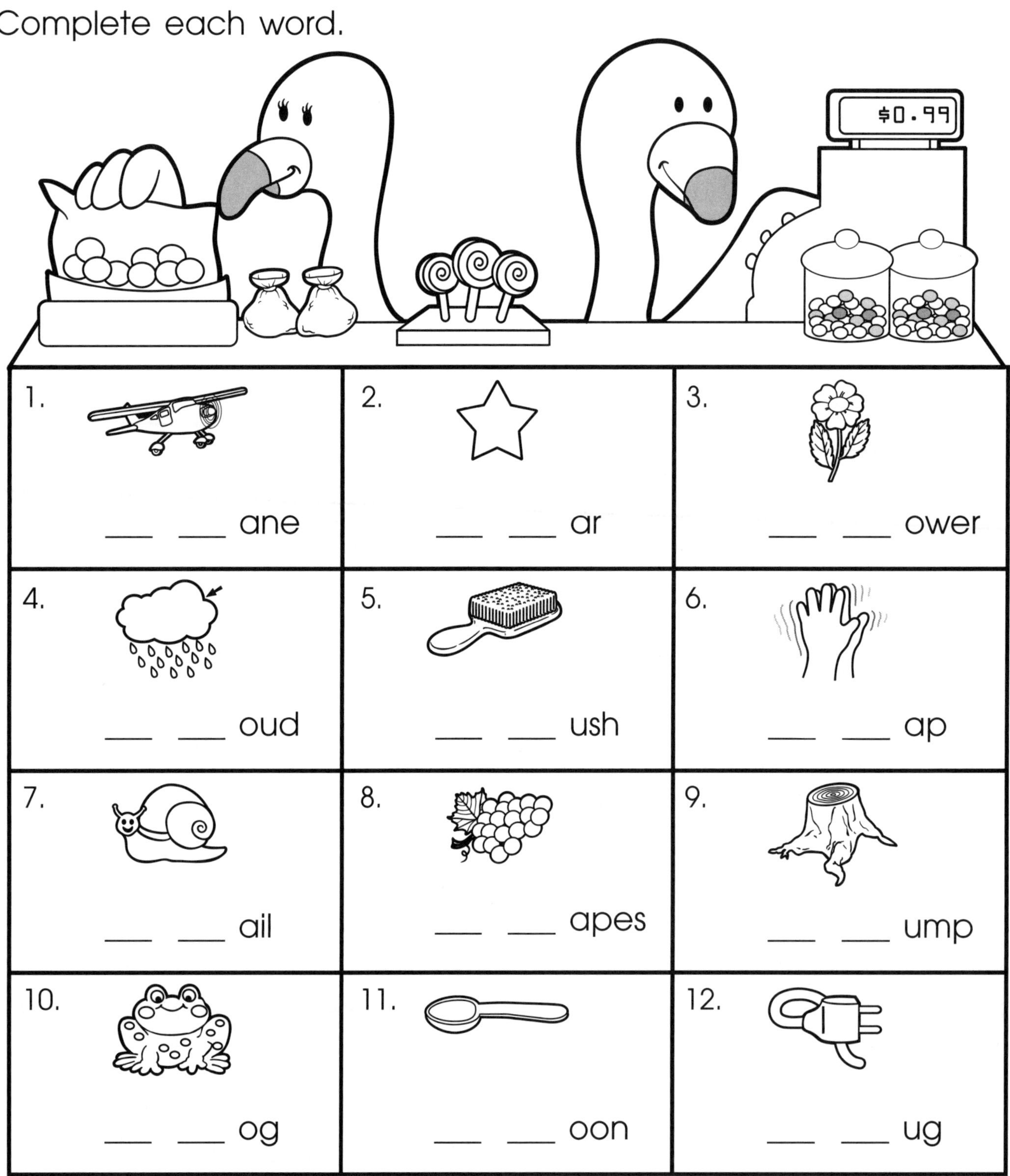
$0.99
1. ___ ___ ane
2. ___ ___ ar
3. ___ ___ ower
4. ___ ___ oud
5. ___ ___ ush
6. ___ ___ ap
7. ___ ___ ail
8. ___ ___ apes
9. ___ ___ ump
10. ___ ___ og
11. ___ ___ oon
12. ___ ___ ug

Bonus Box: Circle two of the words above. Use them in sentences on the back of this paper.

Name____

Heading Home

Complete each sentence with a word from the word bank.

LIVE BAIT
Word Bank
stick
sponge
sky
star
skillet
spill

1. Do not ________________ the pail of worms!

2. I will use a ________________ to pick up that worm.

3. Will you wipe up the water with a ________________?

4. The ________________ is getting very dark.

5. There is a bright ________________ in the sky.

6. Let's go and cook dinner in the ________________.

Bonus Box: On the back of this sheet, write other words that begin with **sk, sp,** and **st.**

Name ____

Daydreaming

Color the fish by the code.

LIVE BAIT

Color Code

cr as in —orange

dr as in  —yellow

tr as in —red

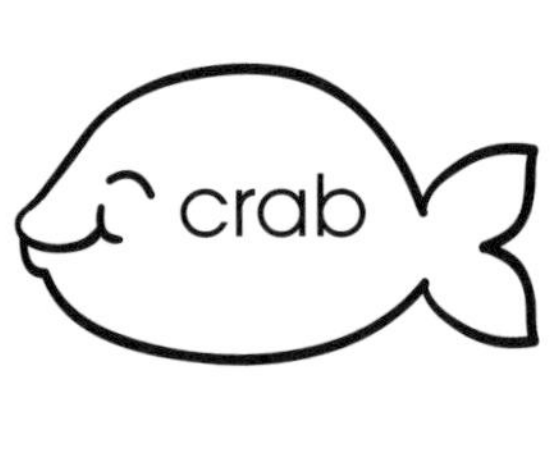
crab

trail
tree

drink

crack

dream

Complete each sentence with a word from above.

1. Let's take a nap under the shady ______________.
2. Have a cool ______________ of water first.
3. Watch out for the ______________ with its claws.
4. I hope the boat does not get a ______________.
5. When we wake up, we can walk on the ______________.
6. What did you ______________ about?

The Best of Teacher's Helper® *Phonics* • ©The Mailbox® Books • TEC61239 • Key p. 126

Name____________________

Fishing Fun

Cut. Glue to match beginning sounds.
Write the word. Use the word bank.

Word Bank		
sled	clam	plug
plant	slide	clown

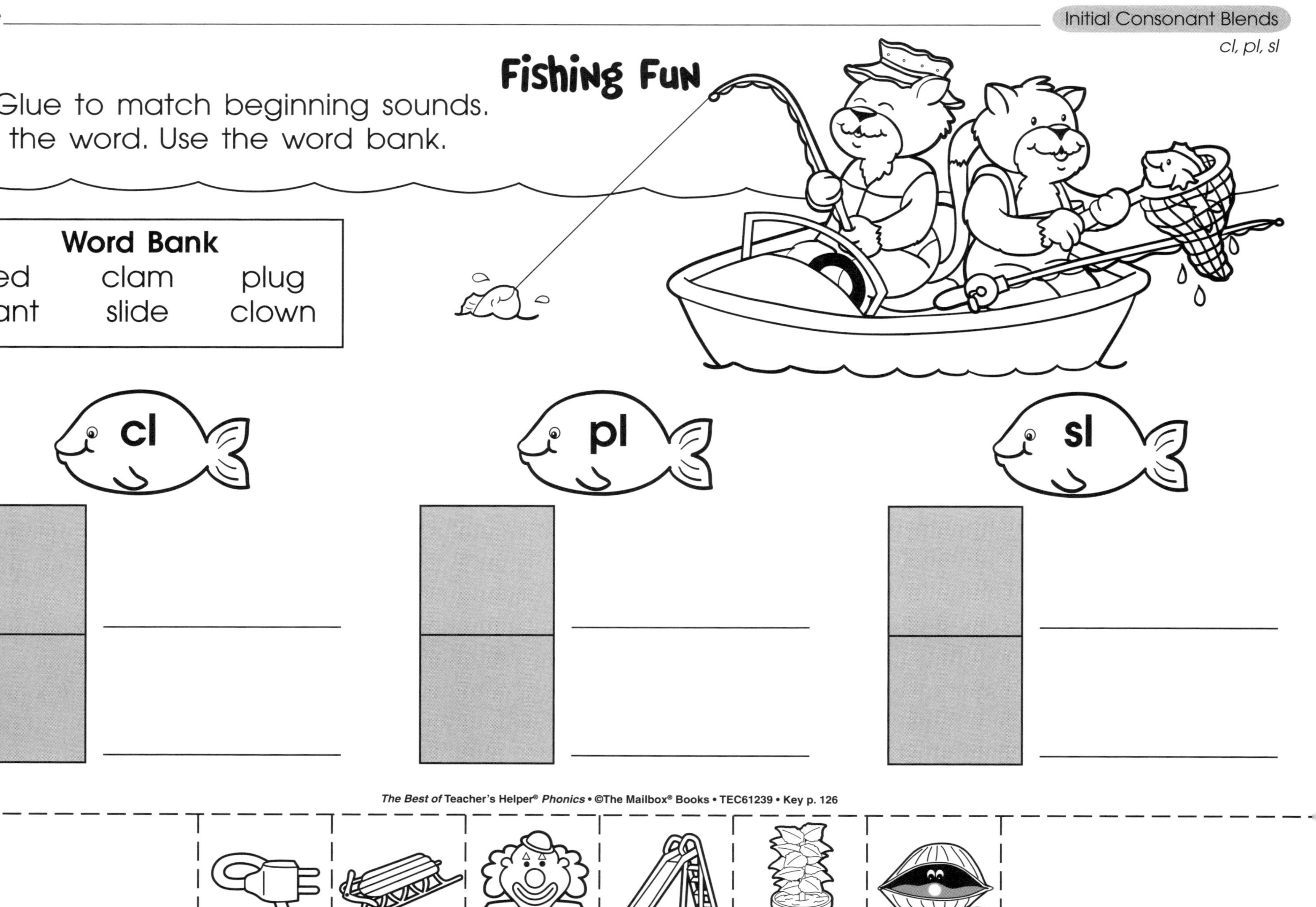
cl
pl
sl

Name________________________________

Initial Consonant Blends
cl, pl, sl

Under Construction

Cut. Glue.
Write each word.

cl

pl

sl

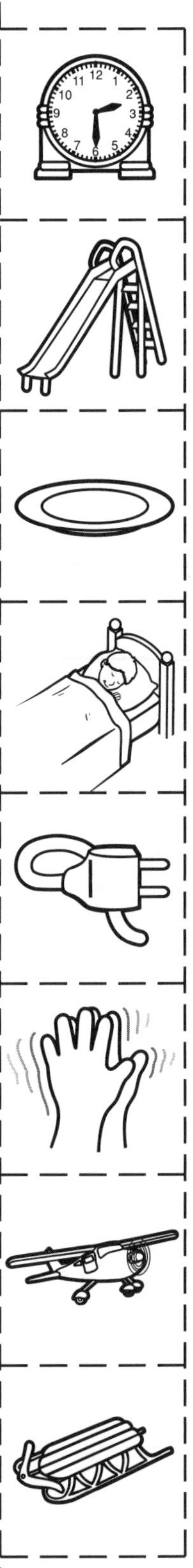

The Best of Teacher's Helper® *Phonics* • ©The Mailbox® Books • TEC61239 • Key p. 126

Name ______________________________________

Plenty of Paint

Color the paint buckets by the code.

Color Code
cr — orange
dr — yellow
tr — green

Write each word below the correct paintbrush.

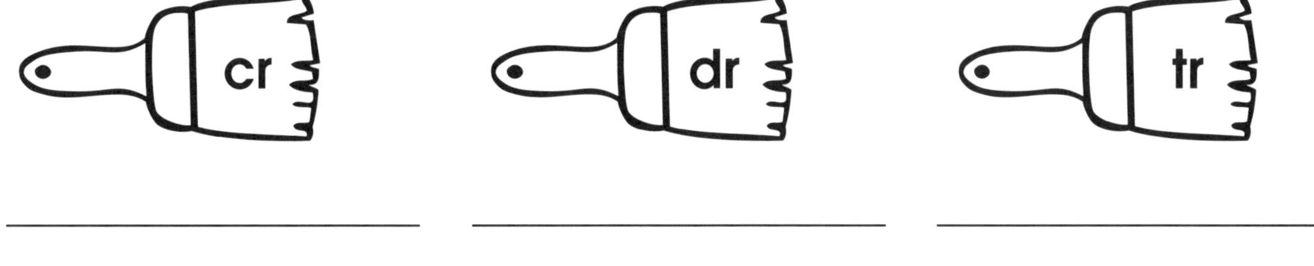
cr
dr
tr

______	______	______
______	______	______
______	______	______
______	______	______

Bonus Box: Circle one word in each list above. Use each word in a sentence on the back of this paper.

 Name____________________

The Finishing Touches

Color each box by the code.

Color Code

sk—red **st**—yellow
sl—blue **sw**—orange

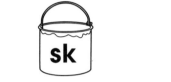

Now write each word below the correct paint bucket.

sk

____
____
____

sl

____
____
____

st

____
____
____

sw

____
____
____

Bonus Box: Choose one group of words from above. Use each word in a sentence on the back of this paper.

Name____

Tea for Tigers

Write **st** to complete each word.
Cut. Glue to match.

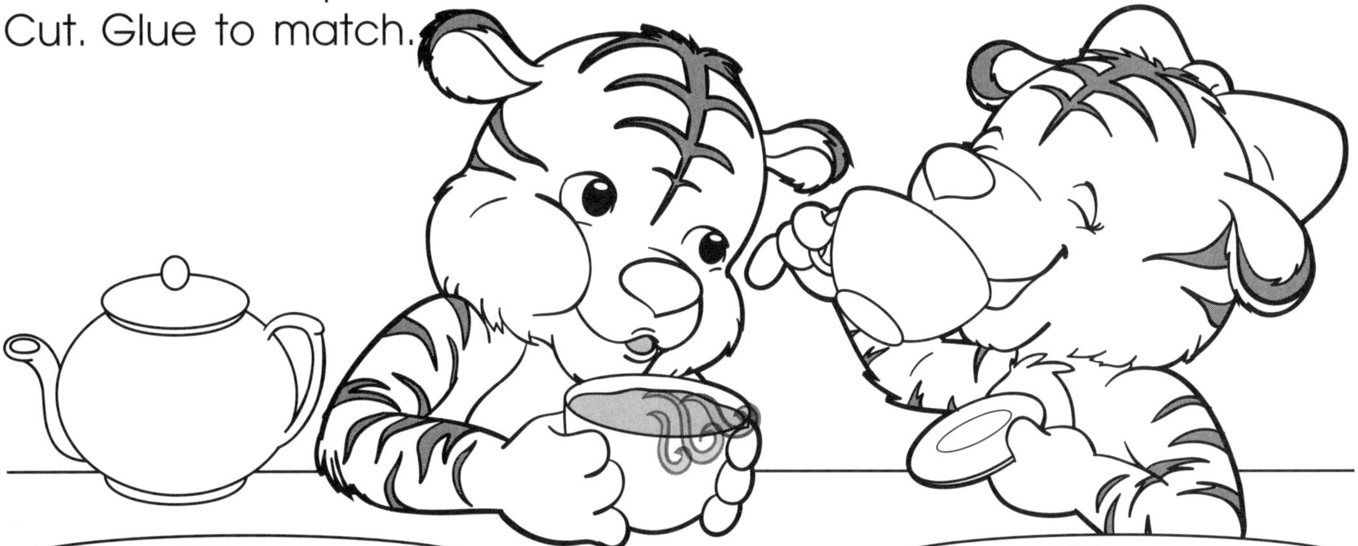

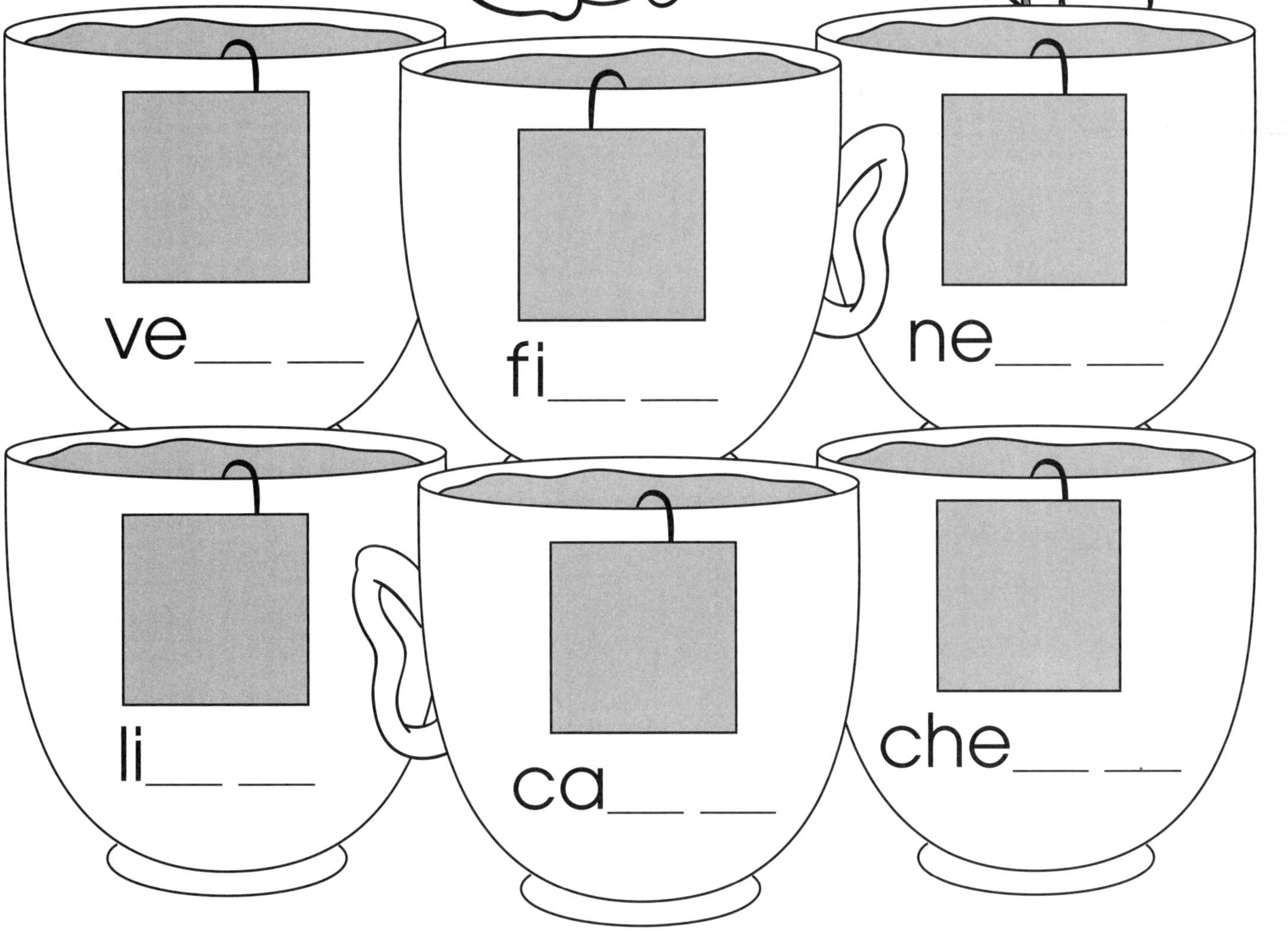

ve__ __

fi__ __

ne__ __

li__ __

ca__ __

che__ __

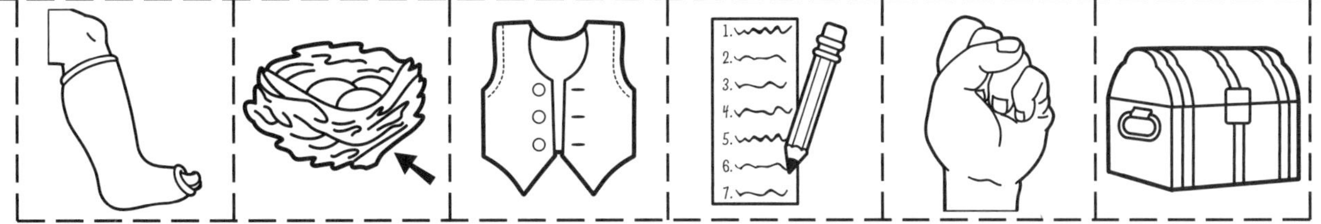

Name____

Afternoon Tea

Use a word from the word bank to complete each sentence.

Word Bank

rest	last	vest	cost
list	best	must	fast

1. I have a ______________ of things I need to buy.

2. How much did the teapot ______________?

3. Don't pour the tea too ______________.

4. This is the ______________ tea I have ever had.

5. I ______________ get this recipe from you.

6. Would you like the ______________ of this piece of cake?

7. You spilled something on your ______________.

8. May I have the ______________ cookie?

The Best of Teacher's Helper® *Phonics* • ©The Mailbox® Books • TEC61239 • Key p. 126

Name____

Heart to Heart

Write **nt** to complete each word.

a __ __

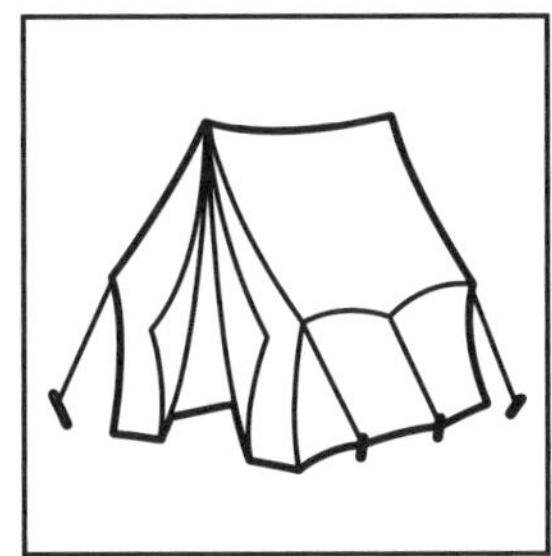

te __ __

pla __ __

pai __ __

Use the words above to complete each sentence.
Hint: Use each word twice.

1. There is a black ______________ on that rock.
2. I am growing a ______________.
3. I want to ______________ my room.
4. The campers slept in a ______________.
5. I bought a can of blue ______________.
6. That ______________ has three leaves.
7. We want to sleep in the ______________.
8. An ______________ has six legs.

Name ____________________

Friendly Cheer

Use a word from the word bank to complete each sentence.

Word Bank

front	sent	spent	paint
hunt	ant	went	plant

1. I ____________________ to the store this morning.
2. I ____________________ a lot of money at the store.
3. I ____________________ you a card.
4. I planted a green ____________________ in my yard.
5. The cat is in ____________________ of the window.
6. I saw a black ____________________ crawling on the ground.
7. That ant will have to ____________________ for food.
8. My dad is going to ____________________ our door red.

Name ______________________________

Teapot Spot

Color by the code.
Write the words below.

Color Code
st—yellow nt—red
pest
bent
ant
cost
hunt
went
test
dust
st
nt

Pretty Pearls

Write **ar, or,** or **ir** to complete each word.

sh ___ ___ t
c ___ ___
h ___ ___ n
st ___ ___
g ___ ___ l
c ___ ___ n
sh ___ ___ k
h ___ ___ se
f ___ ___ k
st ___ ___
b ___ ___ d
y ___ ___ n

Name____________________

All-Star Dad!

Circle the best word to complete each sentence.
Write it on the line.

1. Buddy and his dad like to play in the ____________.

   park   pan   push

2. Dad teaches Buddy to throw the ball ____________.

   fur   for   far

3. Buddy tries ____________ to catch it.

   hurt   hard   her

4. Buddy wants to be a ____________.

   star   stir   store

5. Dad gives Buddy a new ____________.

   shark   shirt   short

6. Dad thinks Buddy will win ____________ prize.

   fork   far   first

Name____ *R*-Controlled Vowels
Short *a, ar*

Wish for Fish

Name each picture.
Color the fish by the code.

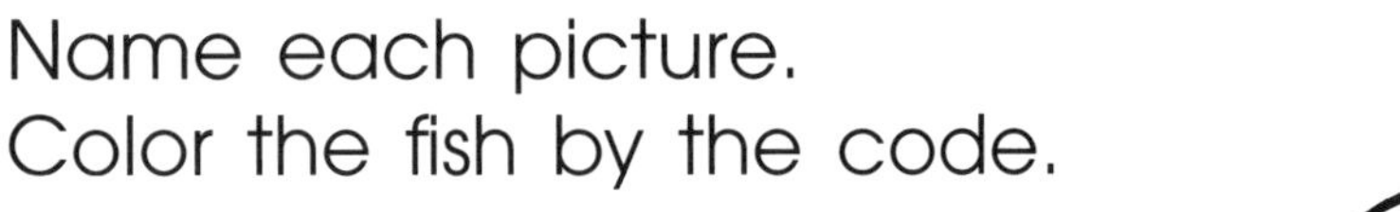

There should be 5 orange fish and 5 yellow fish.

Color Code

short a as in  — orange **ar** as in  — yellow

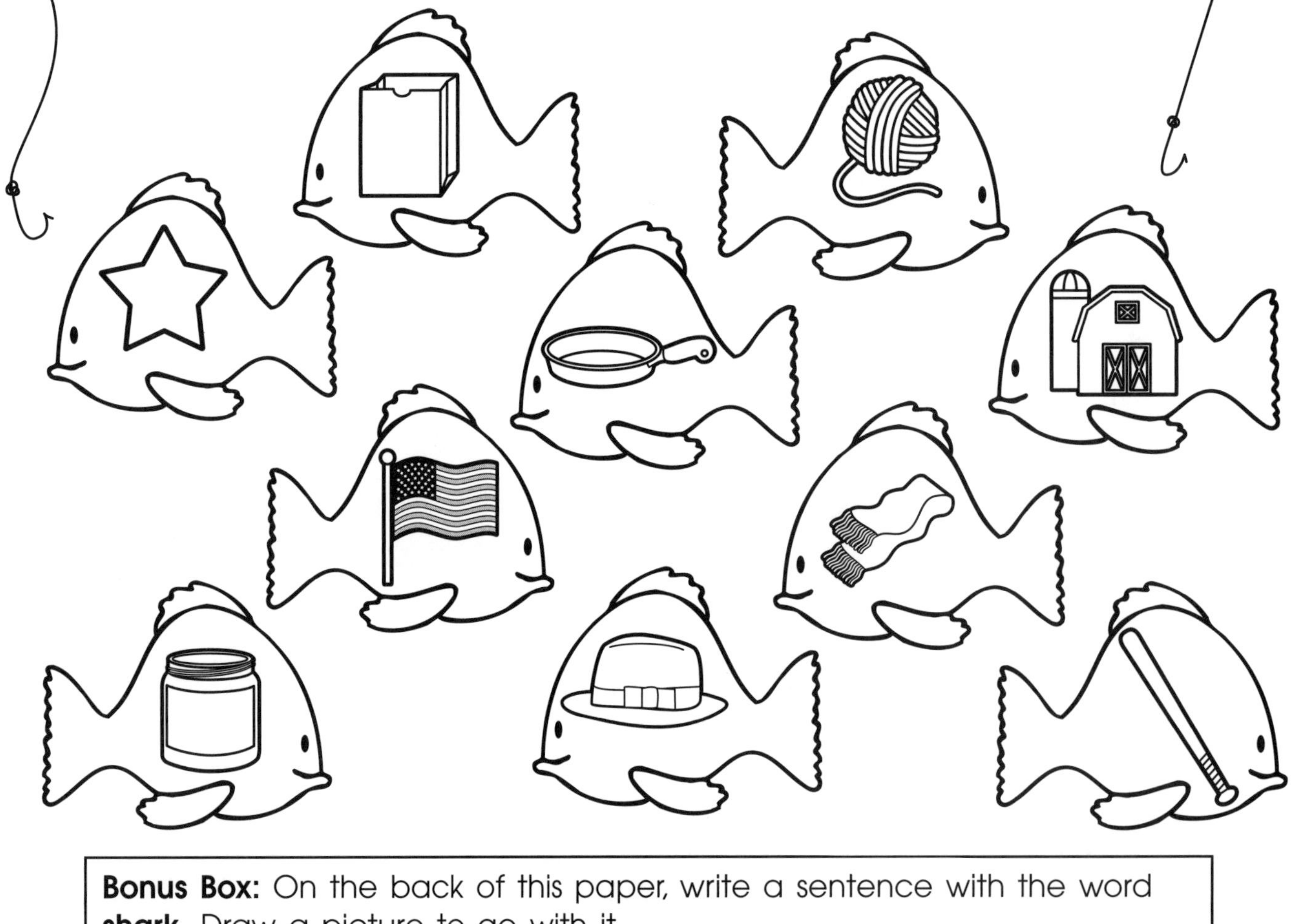

Bonus Box: On the back of this paper, write a sentence with the word **shark.** Draw a picture to go with it.

Name________________________________

Reel It In!

Cut. Name each picture.
Glue to match the vowel sound.
Write. Use the word bank.

short o as in
or as in
Word Bank
box horn
fork top
sock horse

Bonus Box: On the back of this paper, write sentences with the words **frog** and **fork**. Draw pictures to go with them.

Fish Tales

Cut. Glue to match the vowel sounds.
Write. Use the word bank.

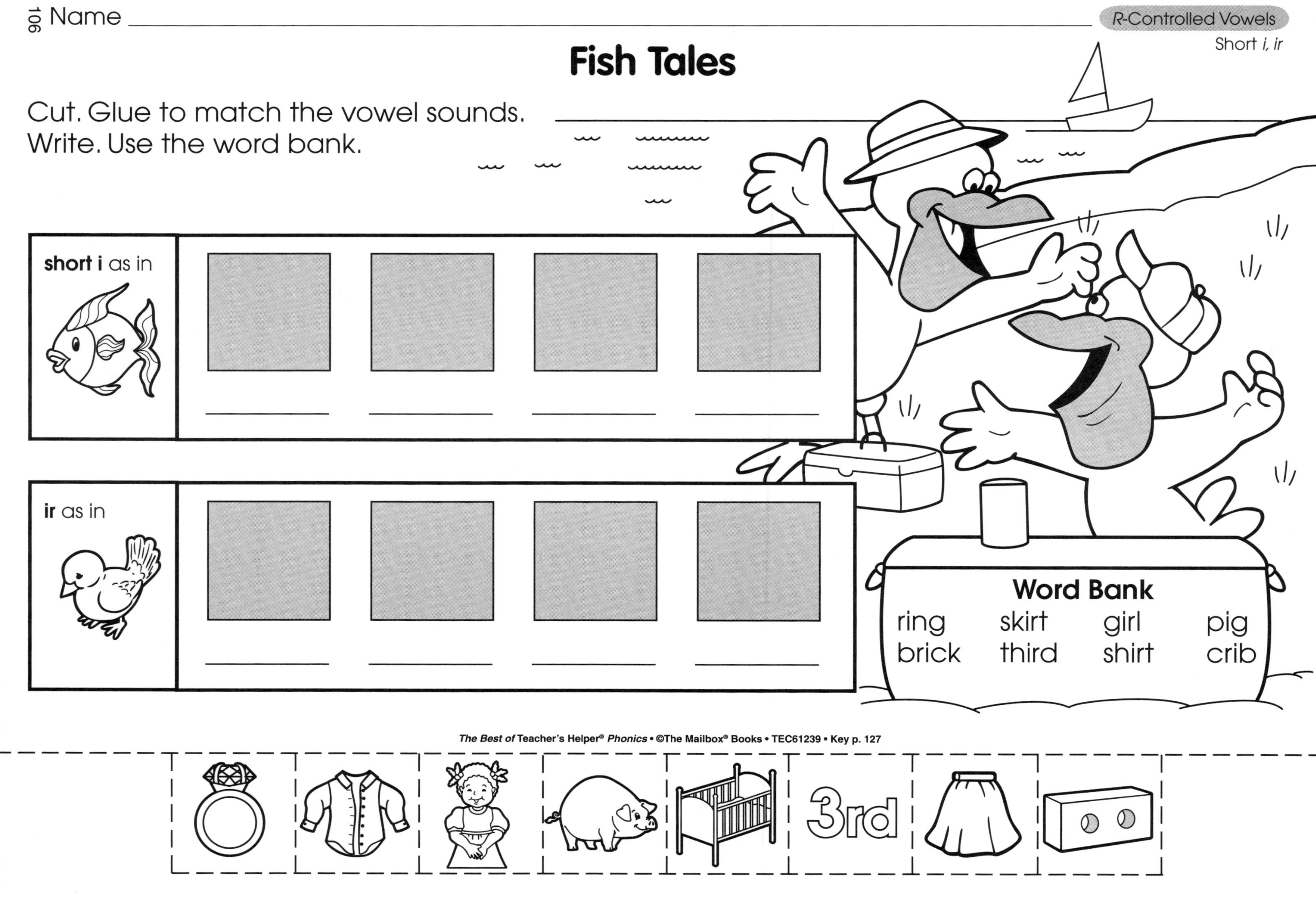
short i as in
ir as in
3rd

Word Bank

ring	skirt	girl	pig
brick	third	shirt	crib

Name ____

It's a Keeper!

Use the word bank to complete each sentence.

Word Bank

water	her	hard	party
dark	far	after	summer

1. Pat likes ______________ new fishing hat.

2. She got the hat at a birthday ______________.

3. The fish could not get ______________ away.

4. The net keeps the fish out of the ______________.

5. Is it ______________ to hold that big net?

6. We will go swimming ______________ we fish.

7. I think it will be getting ______________ soon.

8. It is fun to fish in the ______________!

Name________________________________

A Big Catch

Read the words on the fish.
Draw a line under **ar** or **ur** in each word.
Use the words to complete the sentences.

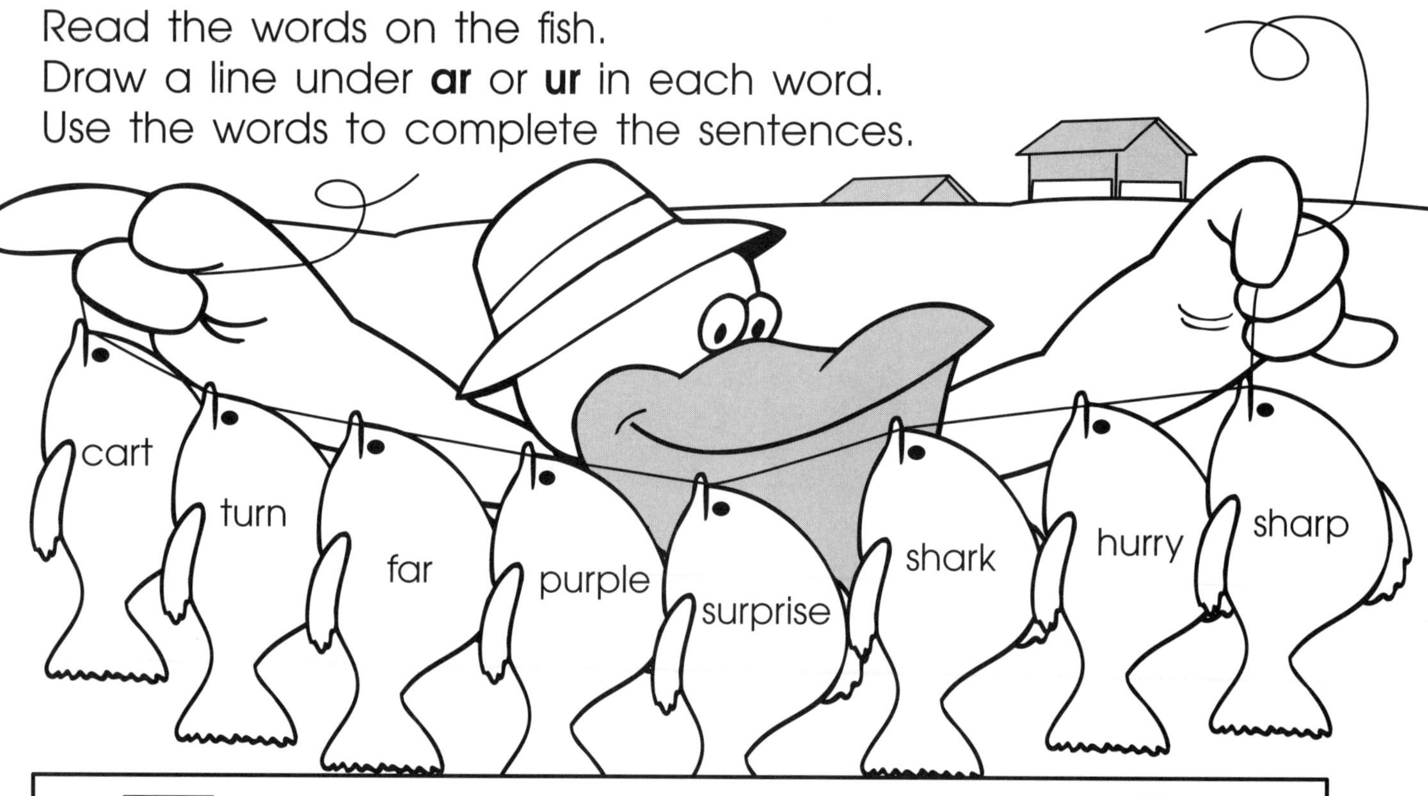
cart
turn
far
purple
surprise
shark
hurry
sharp

1. Today it was Pete's ______________ to go fishing.
2. His fishing spot is not ______________ from shore.
3. Pete got some pretty ________________ fish.
4. He will ________________ to take them home.
5. He needs to take the fish in a ______________.
6. Did he see a ______________ swimming in the sea?
7. Sharks have very ______________ teeth.
8. A shark would be a big ________________!

Bonus Box: Read the words on the fish above. Color each fish with an **ar** word green. Color each fish with a **ur** word purple.

Name____

Back to the Beach

Circle the correct word for each picture.

1. stir / star / stop	2. skirt / shot / show	3. first / frog / fork
4. tray / turtle / turn	5. card / crab / corn	6. grill / girl / grin
7. him / hammer / hurt	8. you / yard / yarn	9. there / thorn / this
10. bend / barn / bird	11. turkey / turtle / turn	12. rain / ruler / ring

Name ______________________________

Feathered Friends

Circle the correct word in each box.

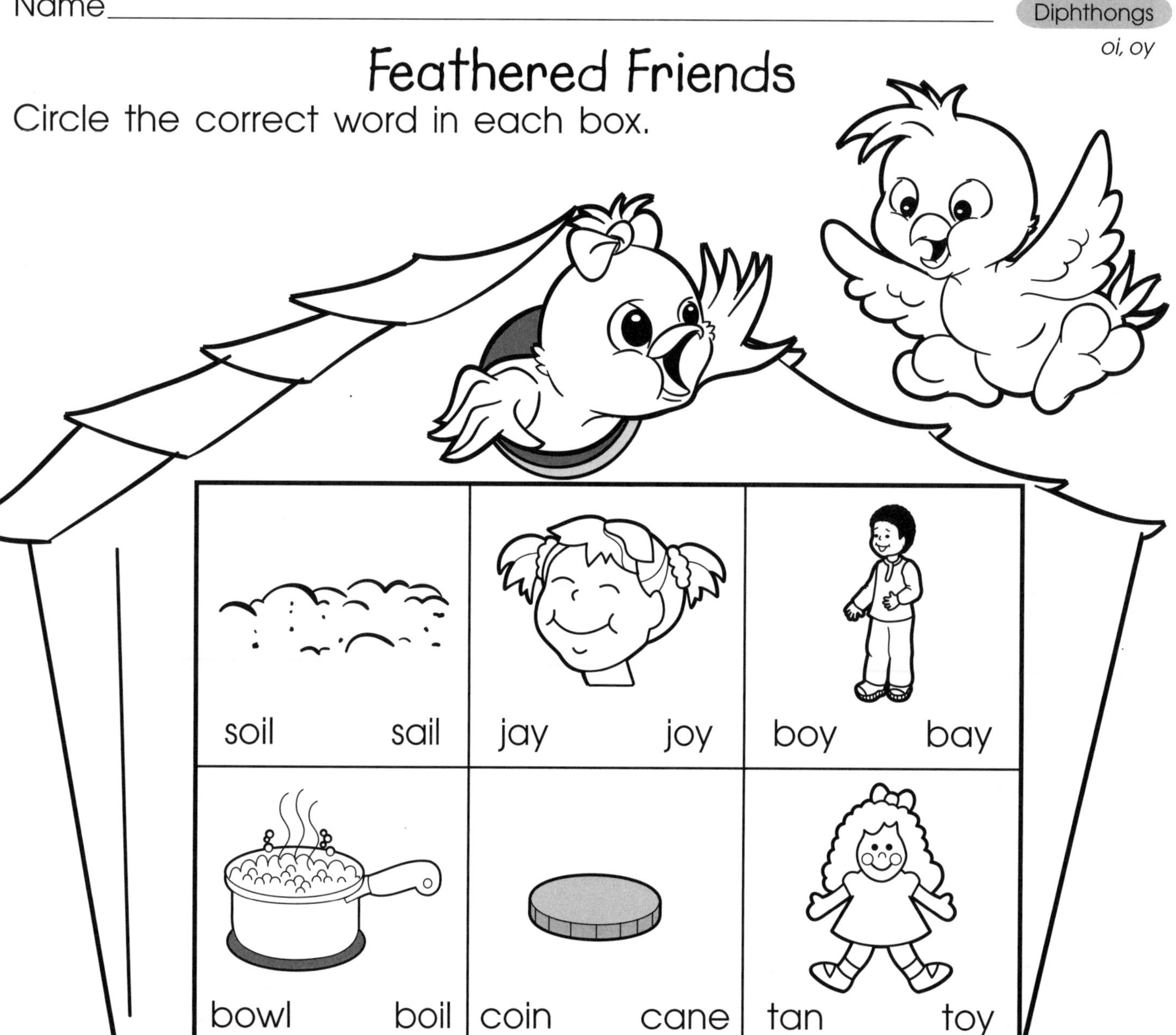
soil sail
jay joy
boy bay
bowl boil
coin cane
tan toy

Use a circled word to complete each sentence.

1. I like to play with this ________________ doll.
2. Did you meet the new ________________ in class?
3. Here is a bag of ________________ for the garden.
4. We jumped for ________________ when we won.
5. I am waiting for the water to ________________.
6. A nickel is a ________________.

Name ______________________________

Early Birds

Write the word that completes each sentence.
Use the word bank.

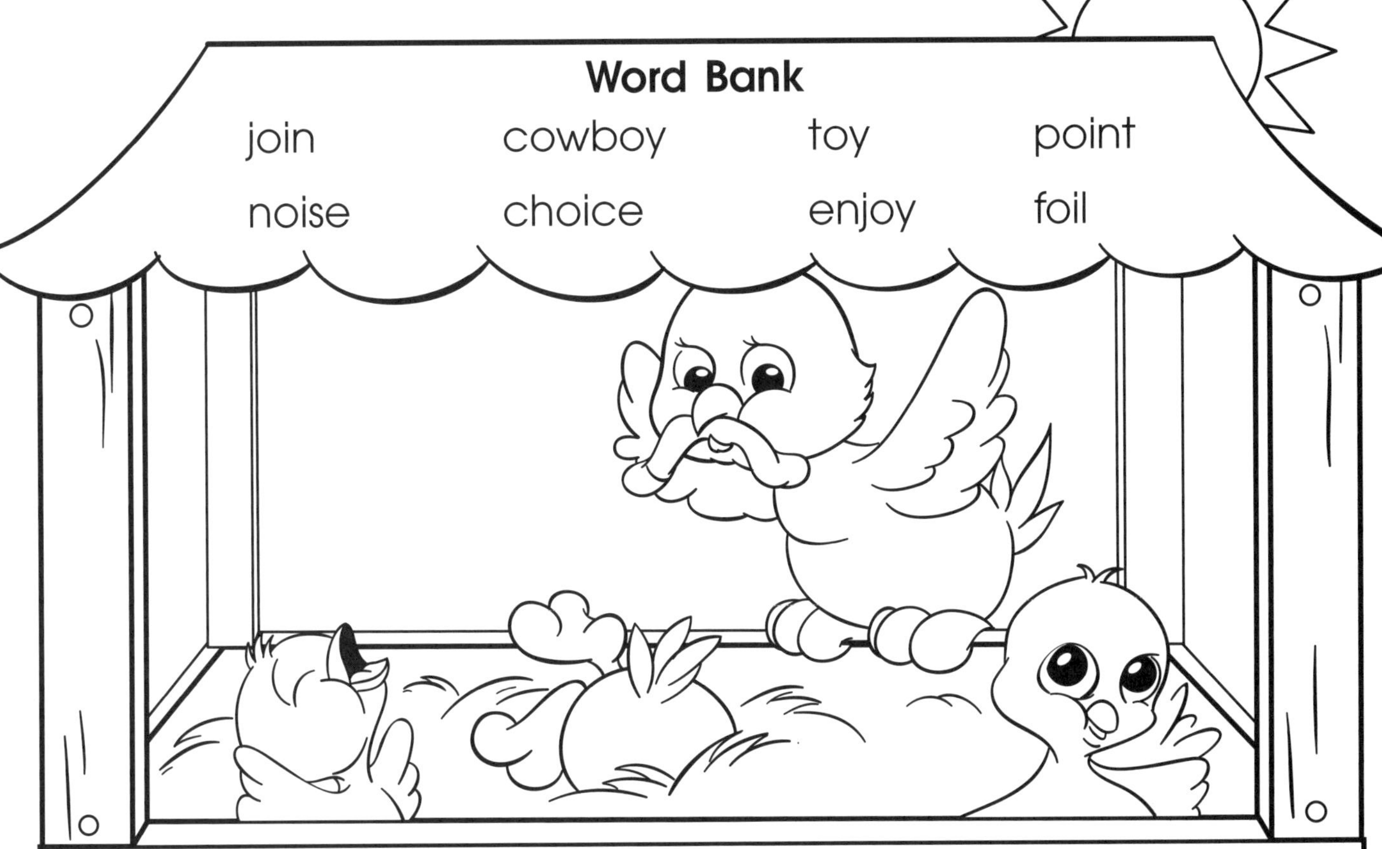
Word Bank
join
cowboy
toy
point
noise
choice
enjoy
foil

1. That ____________________ is riding his horse.
2. Did you ____________________ your dinner?
3. Would you like to ____________________ our team?
4. I got this ____________________ for my birthday.
5. That was a very loud ____________________.
6. My pencil has a sharp ____________________.
7. You will make the right ____________________.
8. Please wrap the meat in ____________________.

Name ________________________

Bird Songs

Cut and glue to match.

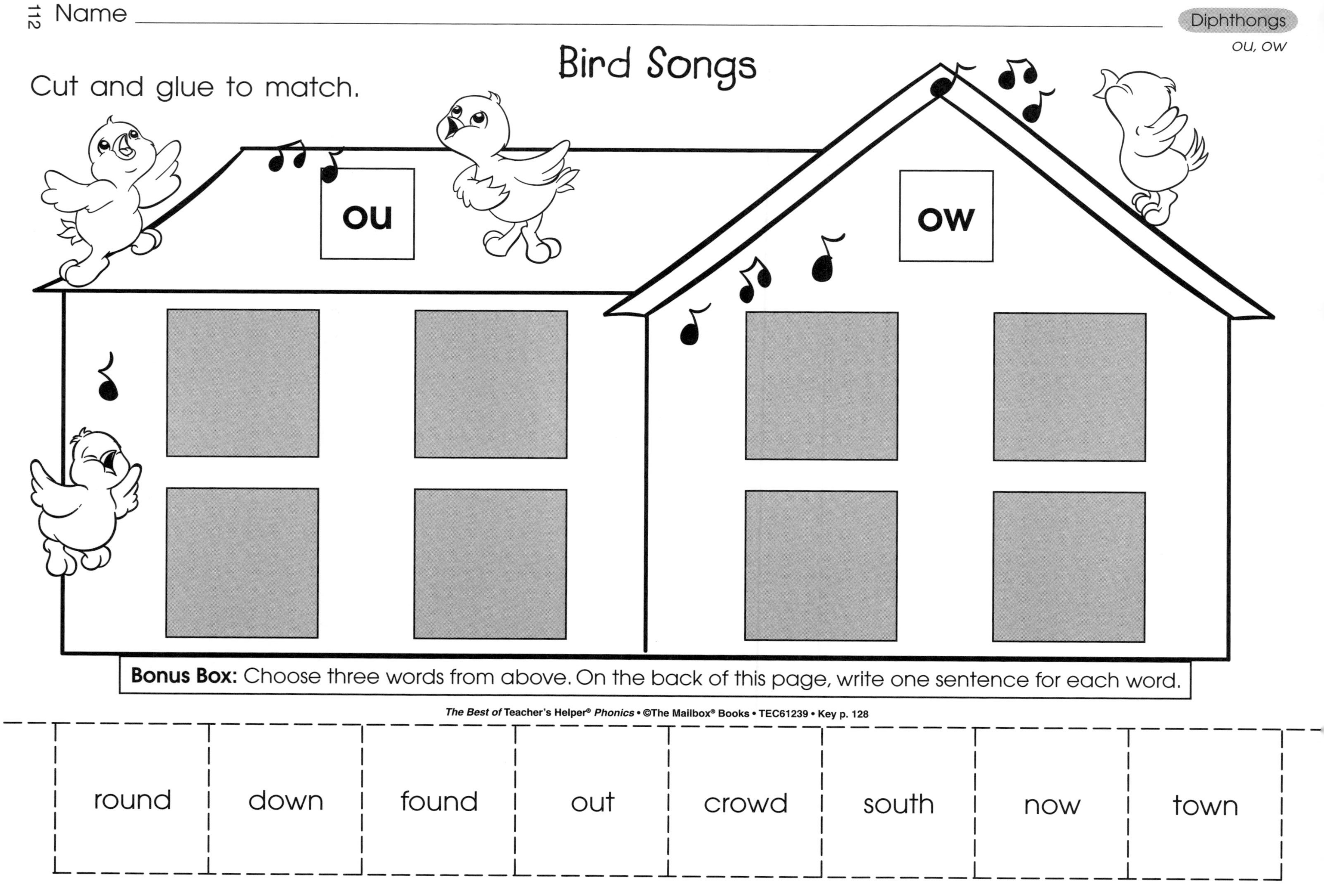
ou
ow

Bonus Box: Choose three words from above. On the back of this page, write one sentence for each word.

round	down	found	out	crowd	south	now	town

Name____

Fly, Fly Away

Write the word for each picture.
Use the word bank.

Word Bank

cloud	couch
flower	clown
shower	mouth
mouse	owl

Complete each sentence with a word from above.

1. I will wash my hair in the ________________.
2. Does your pet ________________ eat cheese?
3. An ________________ lives in that tree.
4. That ________________ is blocking the sun.
5. The hot soup burned my ________________.
6. Mom is sitting on the ________________.
7. Your ________________ garden is pretty.
8. Did you see the circus ________________?

Name ____________________

Sky High

Write the word for each picture.
Use the word bank.

Word Bank

trout cow house
crown towel shout
mouth

____________ ____________

____________ ____________

____________ ____________ ____________

Complete each sentence with a word from above.

1. A king wears a gold ____________.
2. Please do not ____________ in my ear.
3. We saw a ____________ in the lake.
4. My ____________ is next to the bathtub.
5. The ____________ is eating grass.
6. The car is in front of my ____________.
7. Do you have gum in your ____________?

Answer Keys

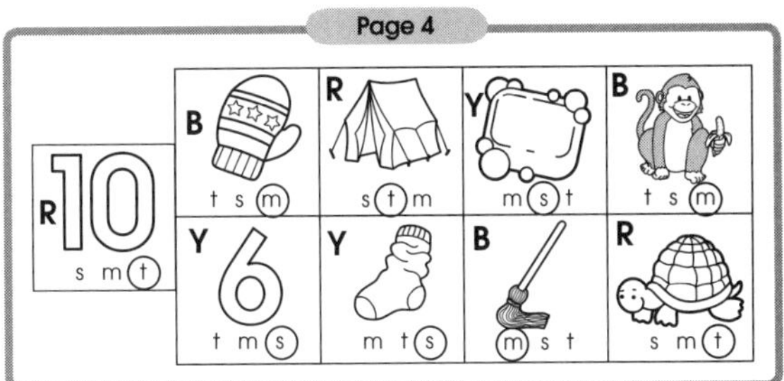
Page 4
R 10 s m t
B t s m
R s t m
Y m s t
B t s m
Y 6 t m s
Y m t s
B m s t
R s m t

Page 5
G r f b
P f b r
P b r f
O r b f
G f r b
O b f r
O r b f
G 5 f b r

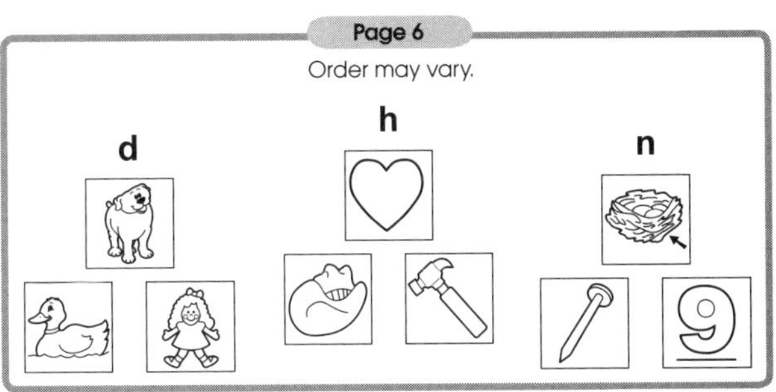
Page 6
Order may vary.
d
h
n
9

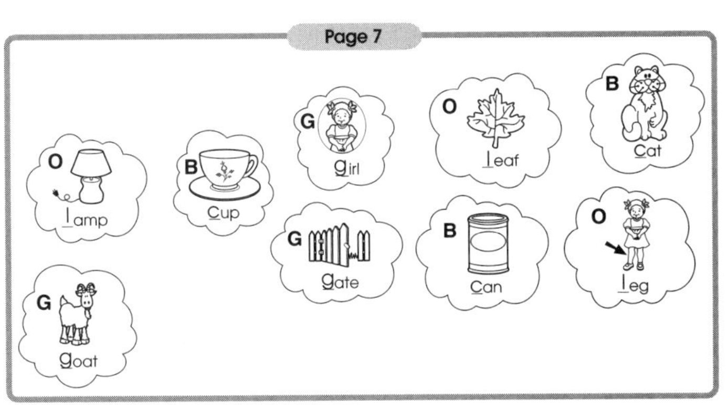
Page 7
O lamp
B Cup
G girl
O leaf
B Cat
G gate
B Can
O leg
G goat

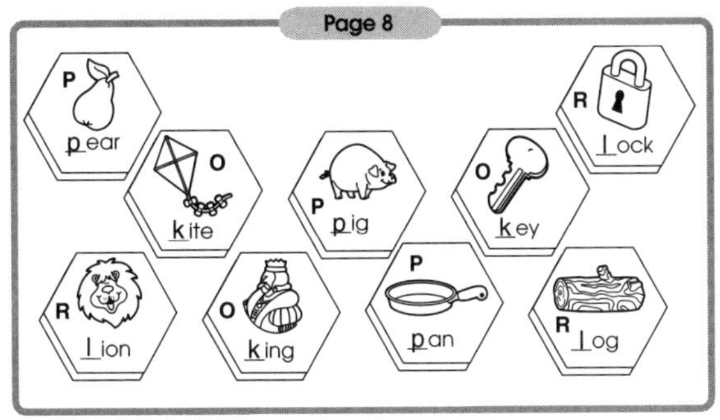
Page 8
P pear
O kite
P pig
O key
R lock
R lion
O king
P pan
R log

Page 9
mouse
top
pail
doll
7 seven
gift
foot
hay
cake
rake
net
lip

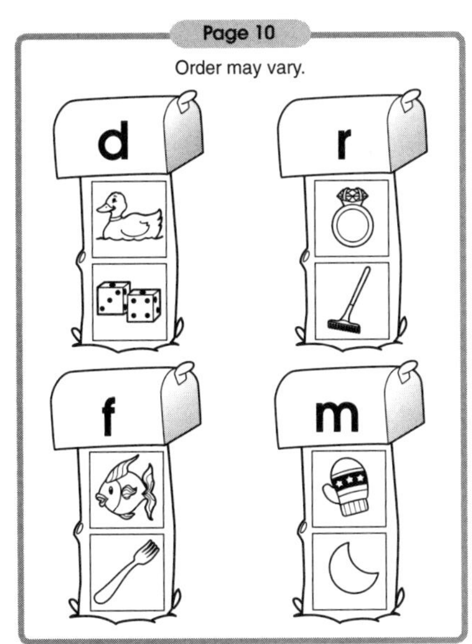
Page 10
Order may vary.
d
r
f
m

Page 11

1. p (blue)	2. n (yellow)	3. v (green)
4. n (yellow)	5. t (red)	6. p (blue)
7. v (green)	8. t (red)	9. n (yellow)

Page 12

Order may vary.

b
j
6
s
k

Page 13

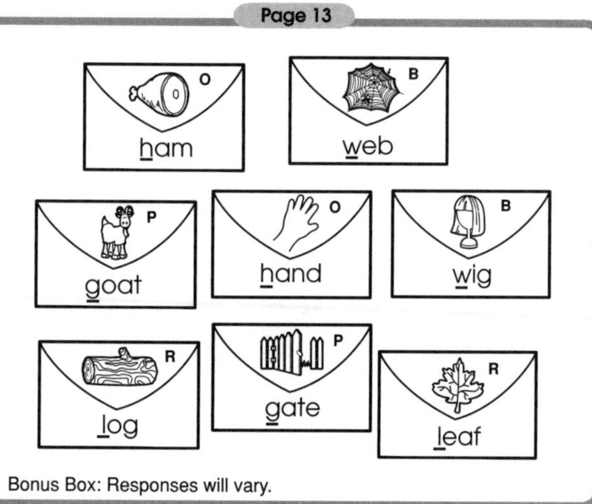
O
ham
B
web
P
goat
O
hand
B
wig
R
log
P
gate
R
leaf

Bonus Box: Responses will vary.

Page 14

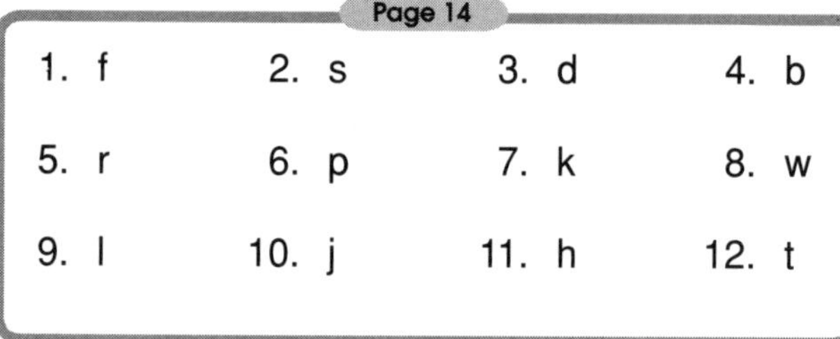

1. f	2. s	3. d	4. b
5. r	6. p	7. k	8. w
9. l	10. j	11. h	12. t

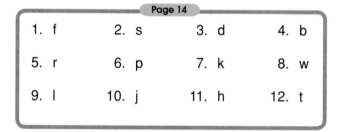

Page 15

Order may vary.

b
m
r
s

Page 16

Order may vary.

g
n
p
t

Page 17

1. f (orange)	2. c (blue)	3. f (orange)	4. h (red)
5. d (yellow)	6. h (red)	7. c (blue)	8. d (yellow)

Bonus Box: Responses will vary.

Page 18

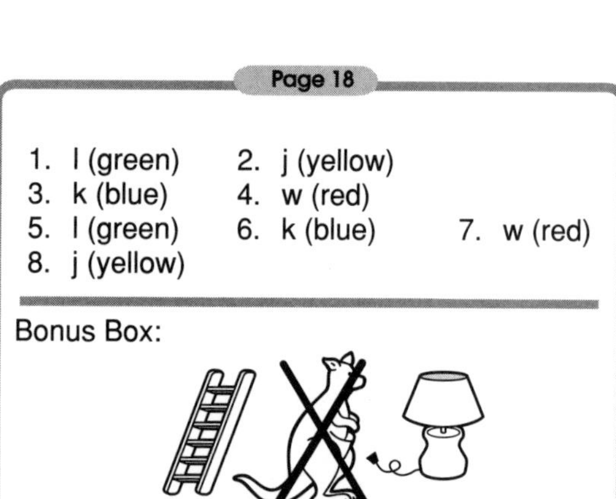

1. l (green)
2. j (yellow)
3. k (blue)
4. w (red)
5. l (green)
6. k (blue)
7. w (red)
8. j (yellow)

Bonus Box:

Page 19

1. k
2. l
3. w
4. j
5. h
6. f
7. d
8. c
9. t
10. p
11. n
12. g
13. s
14. m
15. r
16. b

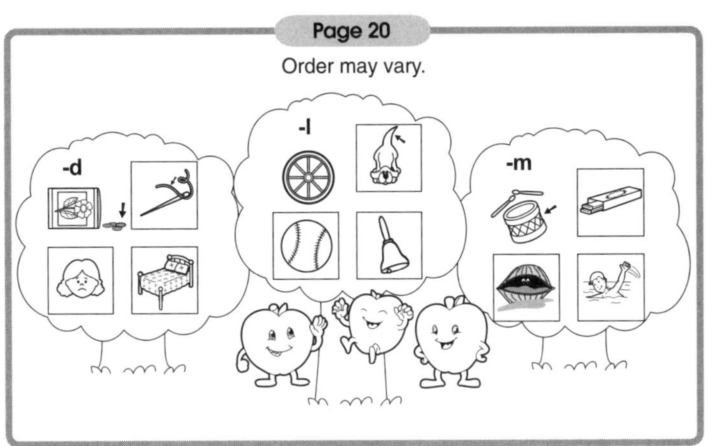

Page 20
Order may vary.
-d
-l
-m

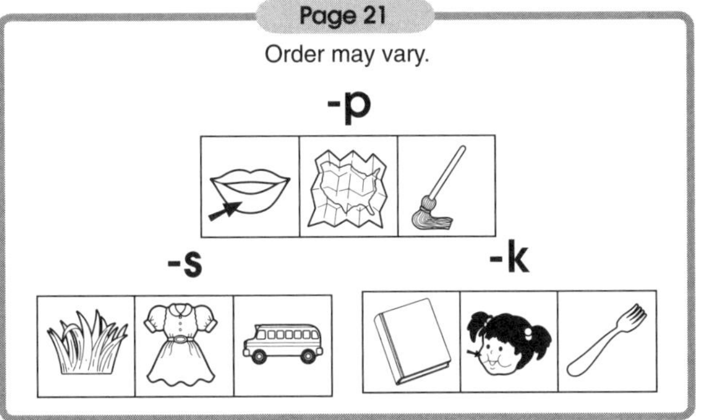

Page 21
Order may vary.
-p
-s
-k

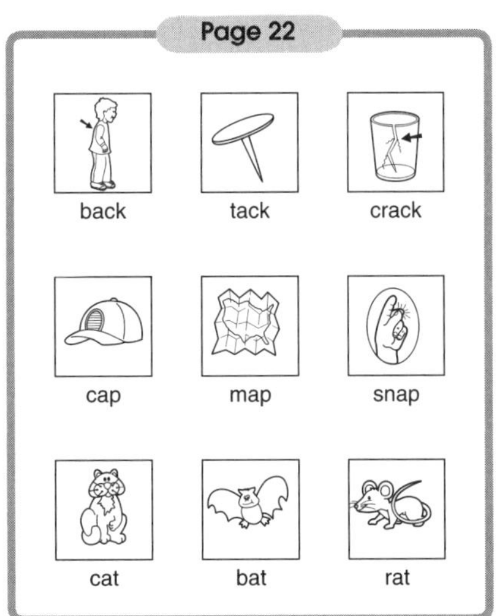

Page 22
back
tack
crack
cap
map
snap
cat
bat
rat

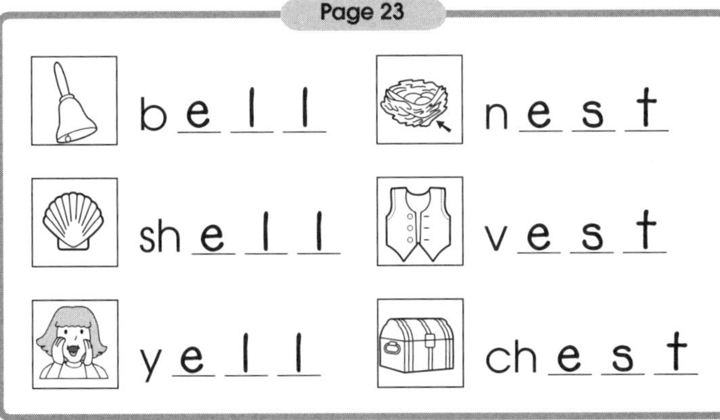

Page 23
bell
nest
shell
vest
yell
chest

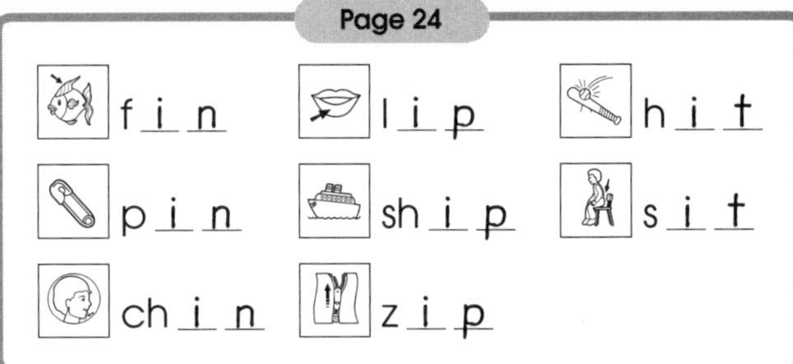

Page 24
fin
lip
hit
pin
ship
sit
chin
zip

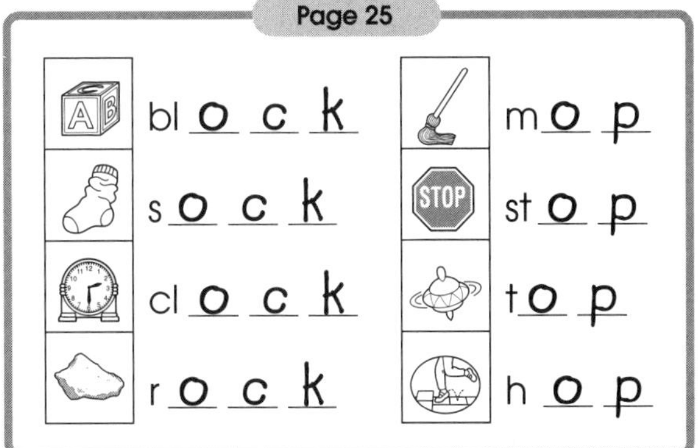

Page 25
block
mop
sock
STOP
stop
clock
top
rock
hop

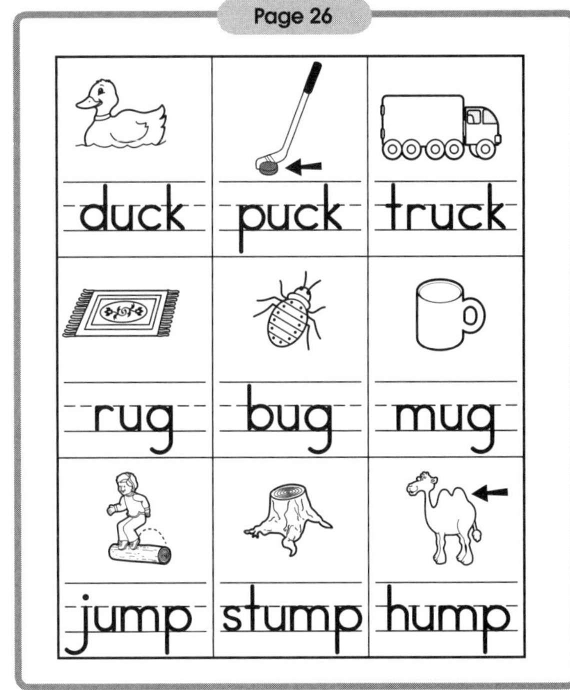

Page 26
duck
puck
truck
rug
bug
mug
jump
stump
hump

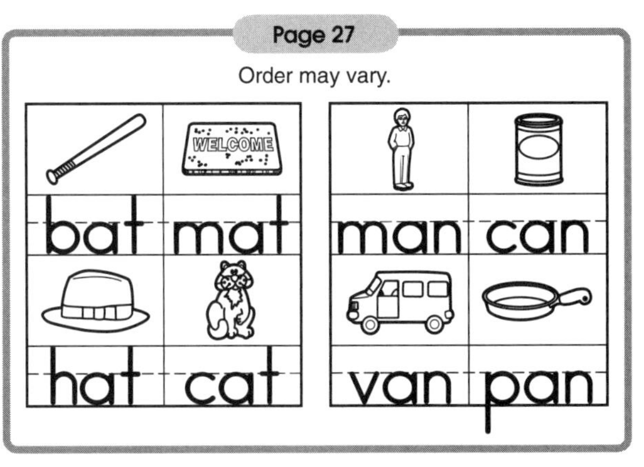

Page 27
Order may vary.
WELCOME
bat
mat
man
can
hat
cat
van
pan

Page 28

Order may vary.

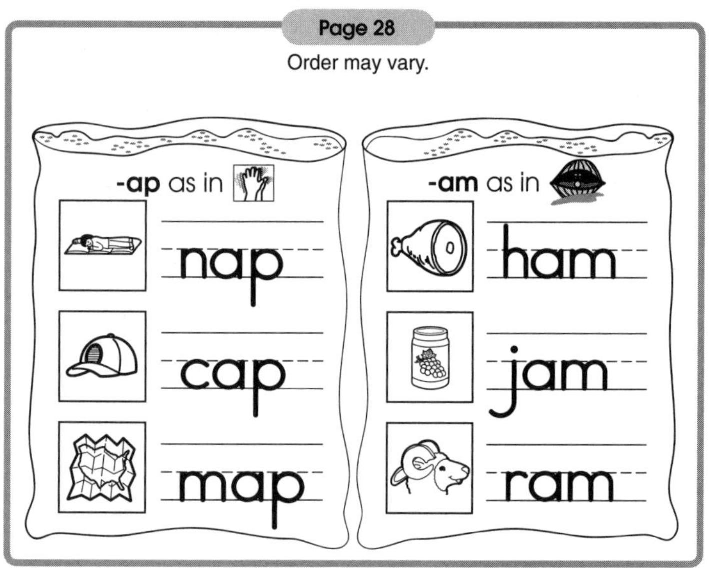

-ap as in
nap
cap
map
-am as in
ham
jam
ram

Page 31

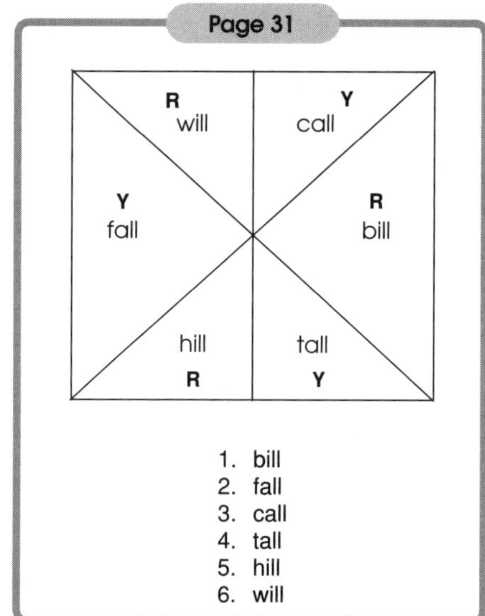

R will
Y call
Y fall
R bill
hill R
tall Y

1. bill
2. fall
3. call
4. tall
5. hill
6. will

Page 29

Order may vary.

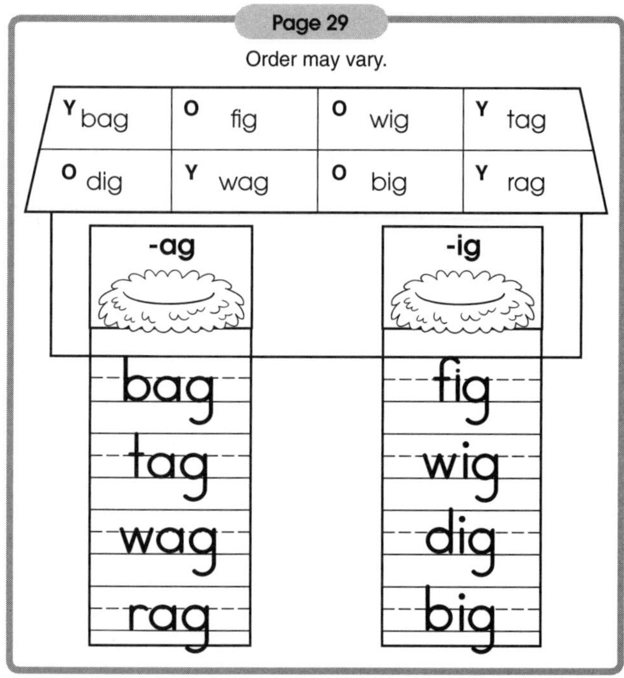

Y bag
O fig
O wig
Y tag
O dig
Y wag
O big
Y rag
-ag
-ig
bag
tag
wag
rag
fig
wig
dig
big

Page 32

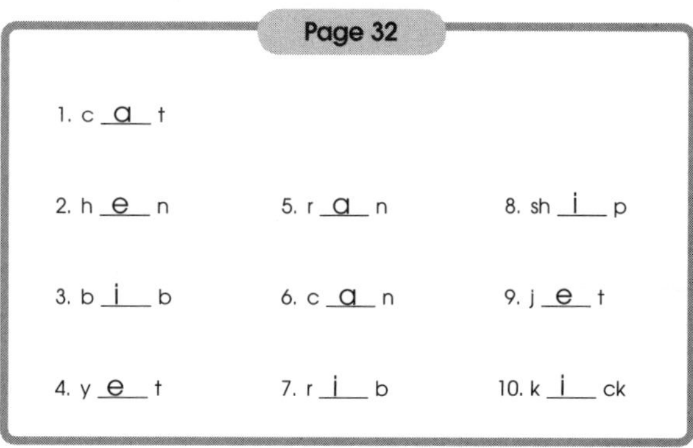

1. c a t
2. h e n
5. r a n
8. sh i p
3. b i b
6. c a n
9. j e t
4. y e t
7. r i b
10. k i ck

Page 30

Order may vary.

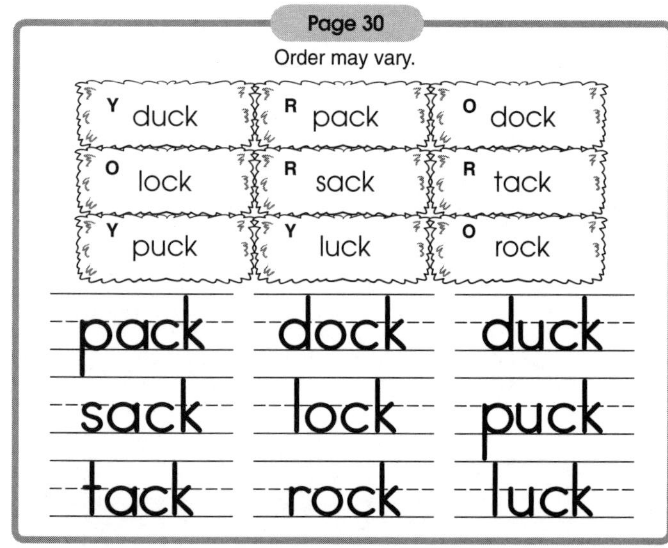

Y duck
R pack
O dock
O lock
R sack
R tack
Y puck
Y luck
O rock
pack
dock
duck
sack
lock
puck
tack
rock
luck

Page 33

Order may vary.

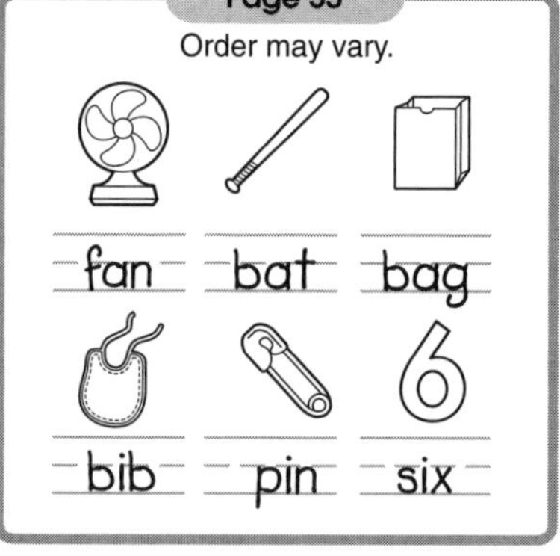

fan
bat
bag
bib
pin
six

Page 34

Order may vary.

O
O
O
Y
Y
Y
O
Y
pan
log
map
top
can
box
hat
mop

Bonus Box: Answers will vary.

Page 35

1. dig
2. top
3. hat
4. hop
5. big
6. pan

Bonus Box: Answers will vary.

Page 36

1. pen (red)
2. sun (blue)
3. web (red)
4. cup (blue)
5. bug (blue)
6. ten (red)
7. bed (red)
8. gum (blue)

Bonus Box: Answers will vary.

Page 37

1. bus
2. mug
3. nest
4. duck
5. pen
6. cut
7. pet

Page 38

Order may vary.

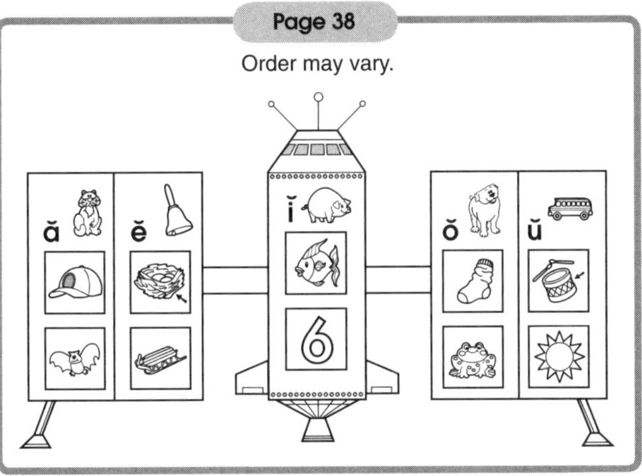
ă
ĕ
ĭ
ŏ
ŭ
6

Page 39

1. hen
2. pen
3. ten
4. men
5. den
6. tent
7. bent
8. cent

Page 40

Order may vary.

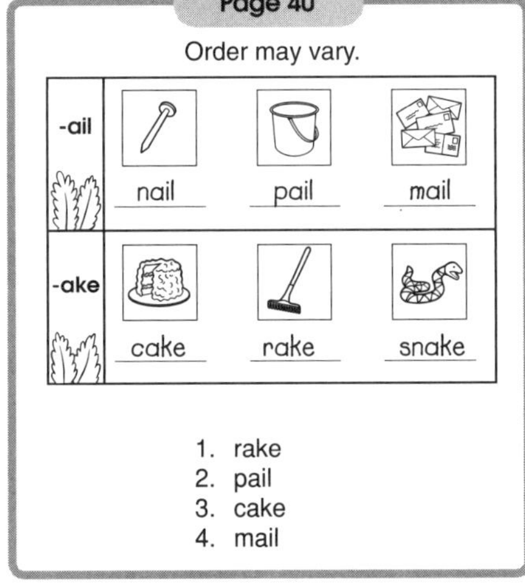
-ail
nail
pail
mail
-ake
cake
rake
snake

1. rake
2. pail
3. cake
4. mail

Page 41

Order may vary.

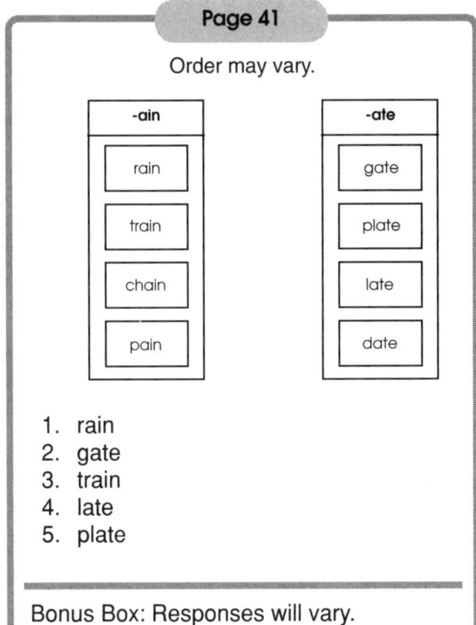
-ain
rain
train
chain
pain
-ate
gate
plate
late
date

1. rain
2. gate
3. train
4. late
5. plate

Bonus Box: Responses will vary.

Page 42

Order may vary.

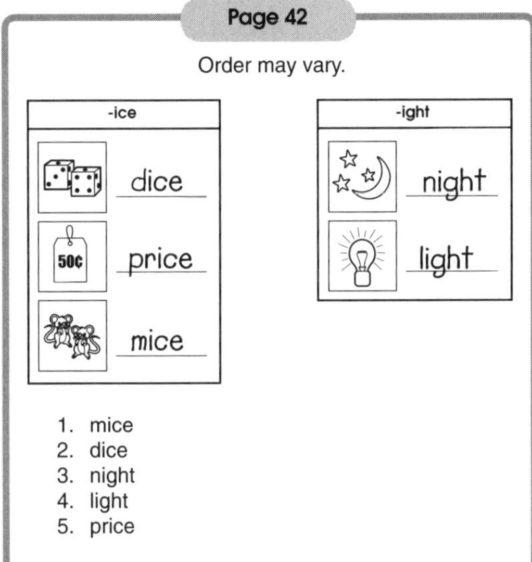
-ice
dice
50¢
price
mice
-ight
night
light

1. mice
2. dice
3. night
4. light
5. price

Page 43

Order may vary.

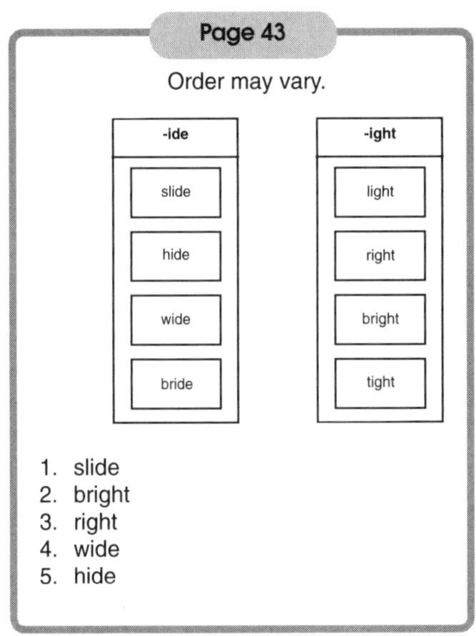
-ide
slide
hide
wide
bride
-ight
light
right
bright
tight

1. slide
2. bright
3. right
4. wide
5. hide

Page 44

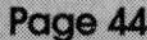

1. rain
2. dice
3. wide
4. make
5. tail
6. rice
7. light
8. shake

Bonus Box: Responses will vary.

Page 45

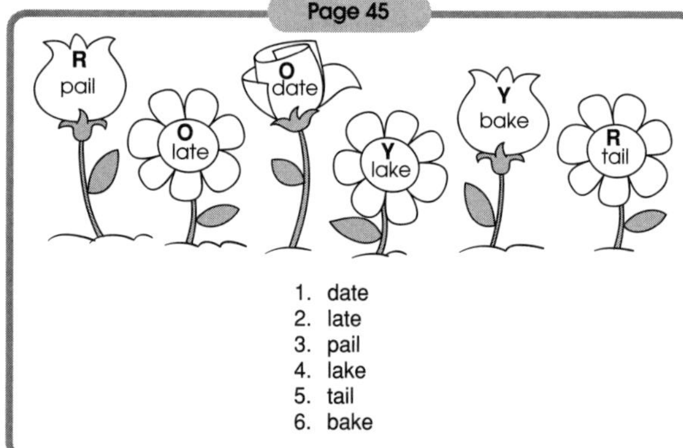

R
pail
O
late
O
date
Y
lake
Y
bake
R
tail

1. date
2. late
3. pail
4. lake
5. tail
6. bake

Page 46

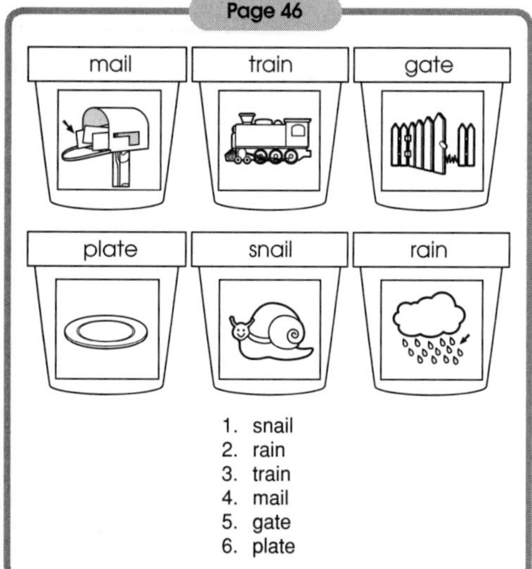

mail
train
gate
plate
snail
rain

1. snail
2. rain
3. train
4. mail
5. gate
6. plate

Page 47

Order may vary.

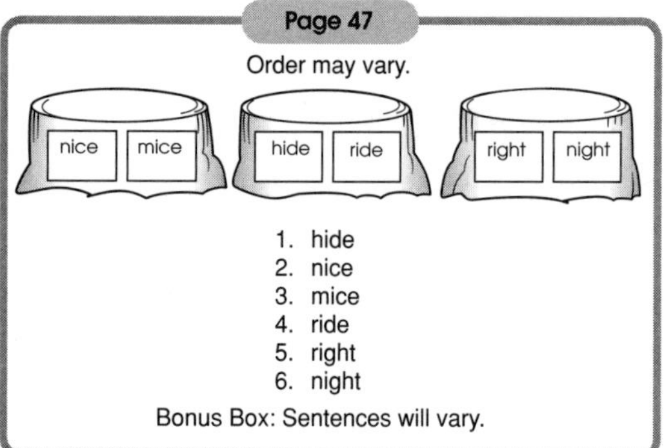

nice
mice
hide
ride
right
night

1. hide
2. nice
3. mice
4. ride
5. right
6. night

Bonus Box: Sentences will vary.

Page 48

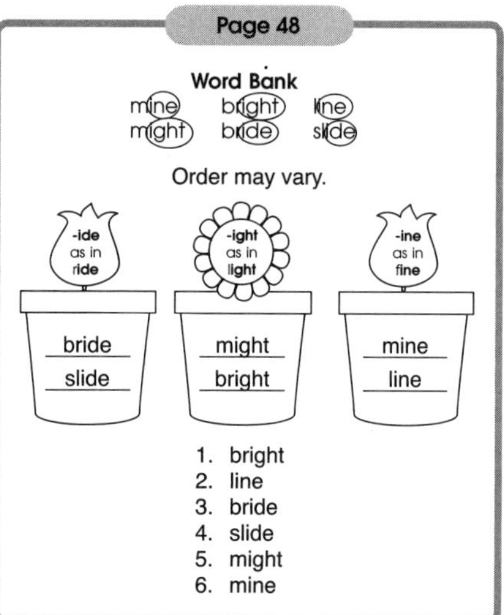

Word Bank
mine
bright
line
might
bride
slide
Order may vary.
-ide as in ride
-ight as in light
-ine as in fine
bride
slide
might
bright
mine
line

1. bright
2. line
3. bride
4. slide
5. might
6. mine

Page 49

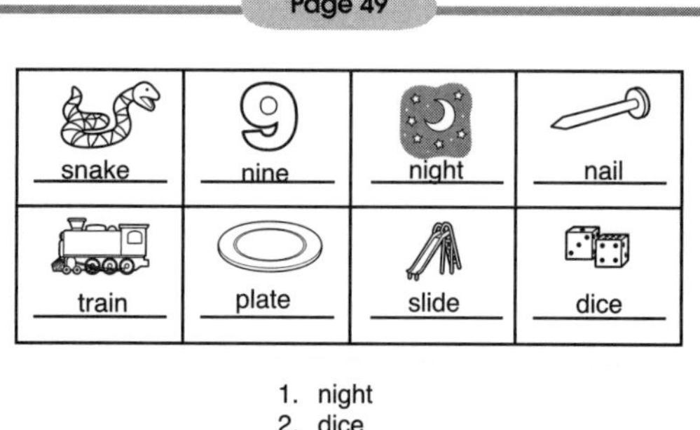

snake
nine
night
nail
train
plate
slide
dice

1. night
2. dice
3. train
4. nail
5. slide

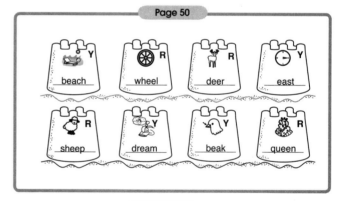

Page 50

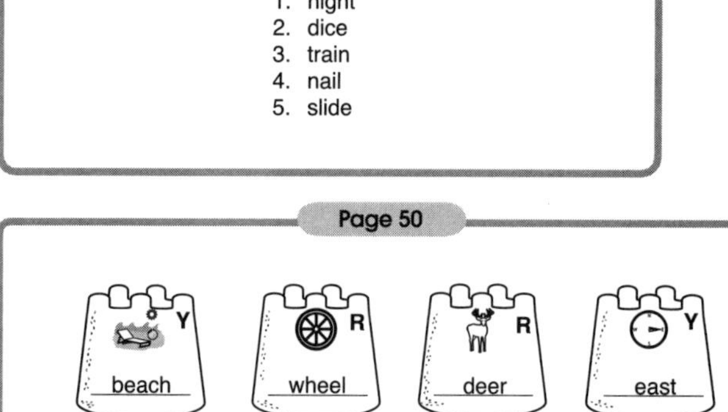

Y
beach
R
wheel
R
deer
Y
east
R
sheep
Y
dream
Y
beak
R
queen

Page 51

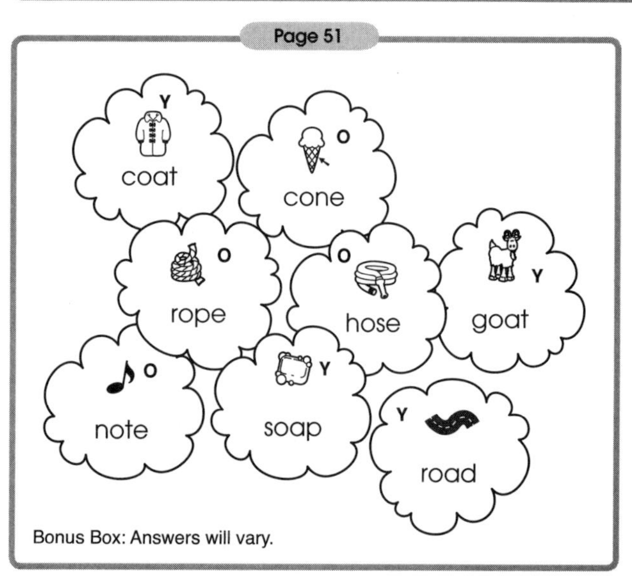

Y
coat
O
cone
O
rope
O
hose
Y
goat
O
note
Y
soap
Y
road

Bonus Box: Answers will vary.

Page 52

Order may vary.

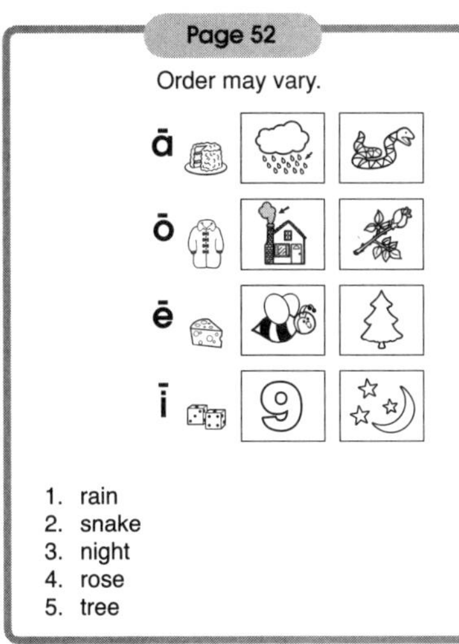

ā
ō
ē
ī
9

1. rain
2. snake
3. night
4. rose
5. tree

Page 53

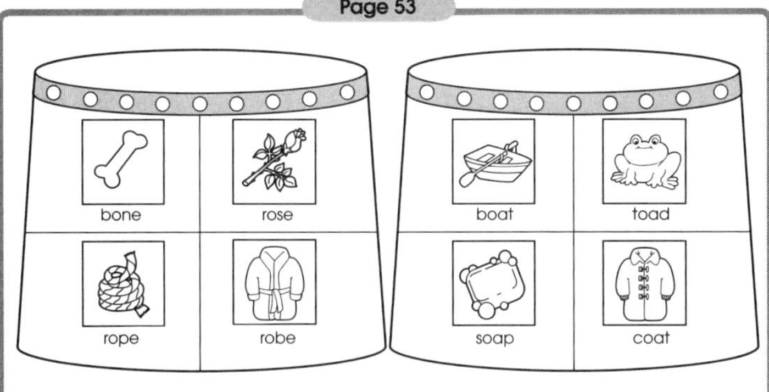

bone
rose
rope
robe
boat
toad
soap
coat

Page 54

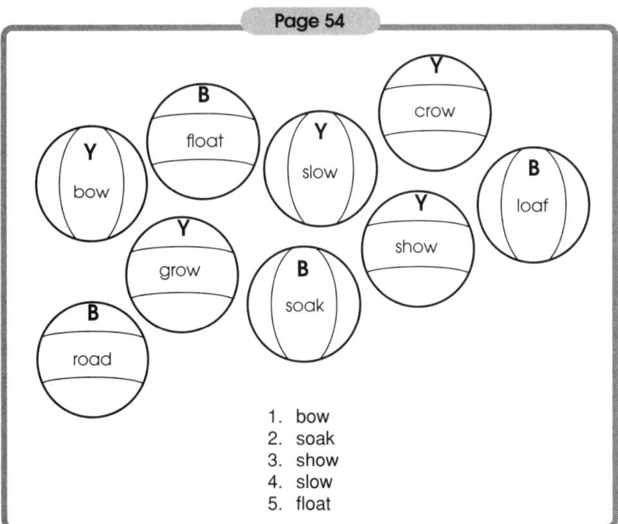

Y
bow
B
float
Y
slow
Y
crow
B
loaf
Y
grow
B
soak
Y
show
B
road

1. bow
2. soak
3. show
4. slow
5. float

Page 55

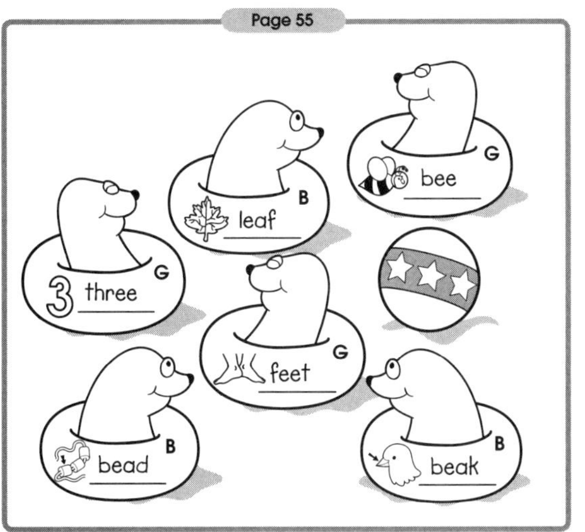

leaf
B
bee
G
three
G
feet
G
bead
B
beak
B

Page 56

1. neat
2. feed
3. eat
4. seal
5. week
6. see
7. deep
8. beach

Page 57

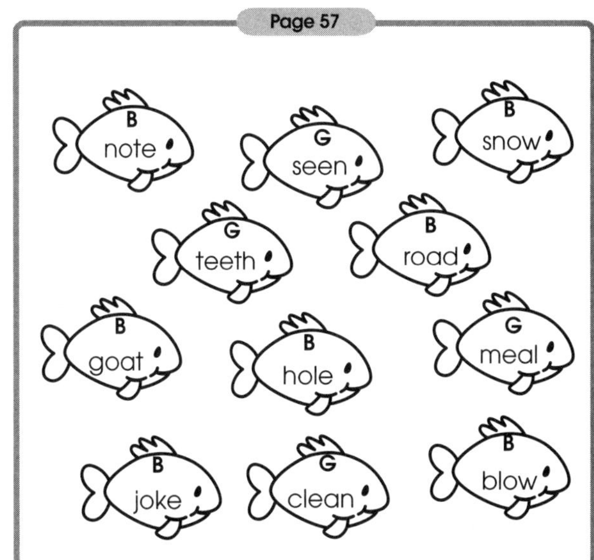

B
note
G
seen
B
snow
G
teeth
B
road
B
goat
B
hole
G
meal
B
joke
G
clean
B
blow

Page 58

pail
cane
snake
rain
tail
gate
cake

Page 59

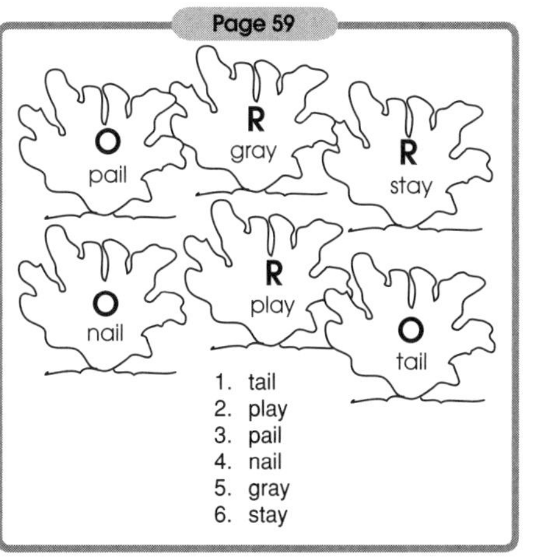

O
pail
R
gray
R
stay
O
nail
R
play
O
tail

1. tail
2. play
3. pail
4. nail
5. gray
6. stay

Page 60

Order may vary.

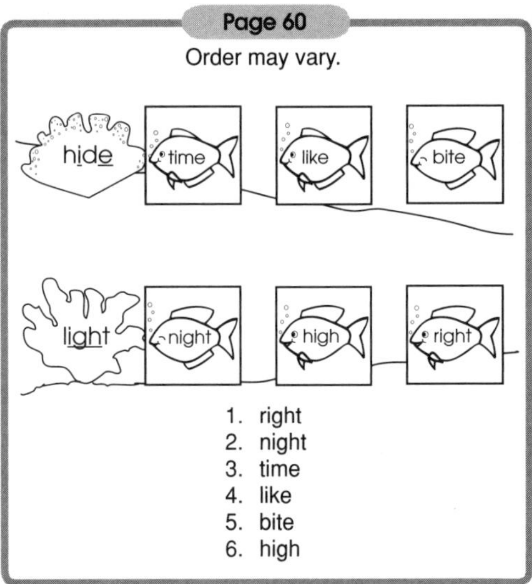

hide
time
like
bite
light
night
high
right

1. right
2. night
3. time
4. like
5. bite
6. high

Page 63

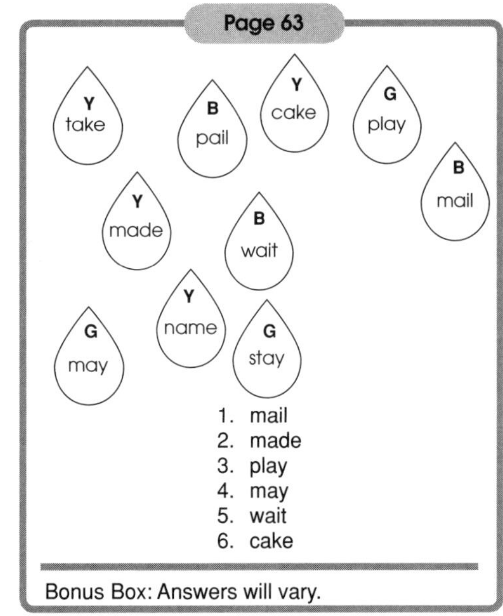

Y take
B pail
Y cake
G play
B mail
Y made
B wait
Y name
G may
G stay

1. mail
2. made
3. play
4. may
5. wait
6. cake

Bonus Box: Answers will vary.

Page 61

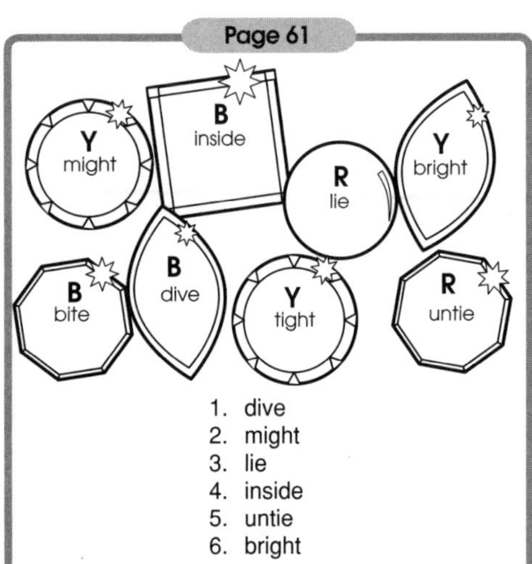

Y might
B inside
R lie
Y bright
B bite
B dive
Y tight
R untie

1. dive
2. might
3. lie
4. inside
5. untie
6. bright

Page 64

Order may vary.

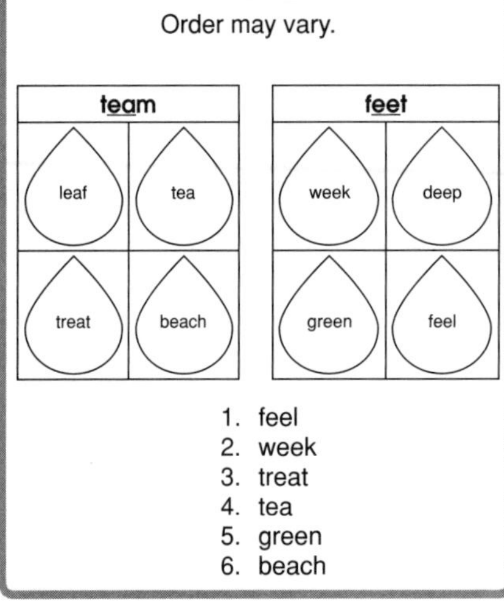

team
leaf
tea
treat
beach
feet
week
deep
green
feel

1. feel
2. week
3. treat
4. tea
5. green
6. beach

Page 66

1. Did I forget my (coat) at (home)?
2. The rain might (soak) me today.
3. I put a (note) beside the (stove).
4. I (hope) we can ride in a (boat) on Monday.
5. It is always fun to (float) on the water.
6. I saw a little (toad) jump on a (stone).

road	bone
coat	home
soak	note
boat	stove
float	hope
toad	stone

Bonus Box: Answers will vary.

Page 65

1. There are many clouds up (high).
2. Mom says that walking in a (line) is (nice).
3. We always turn (right) at the (light).
4. We are going about one more (mile).
5. We (might) get there before (night).
6. Maybe we can (drive) a red car next (time).

dime: line, mile, nice, drive, time

sight: high, light, right, might, night

Page 62

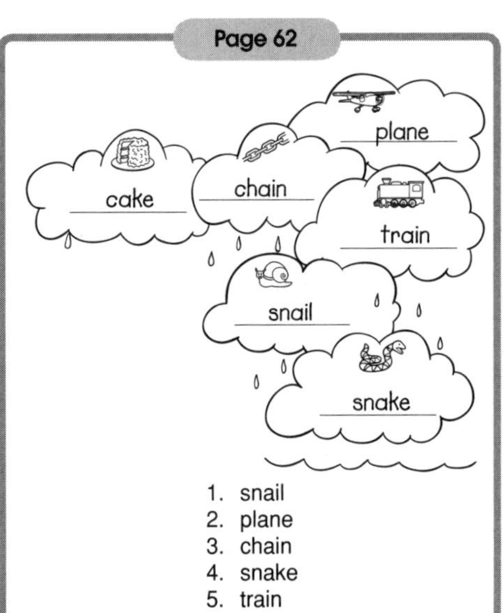

plane
cake
chain
train
snail
snake

1. snail
2. plane
3. chain
4. snake
5. train
6. cake

Page 67

Order may vary.

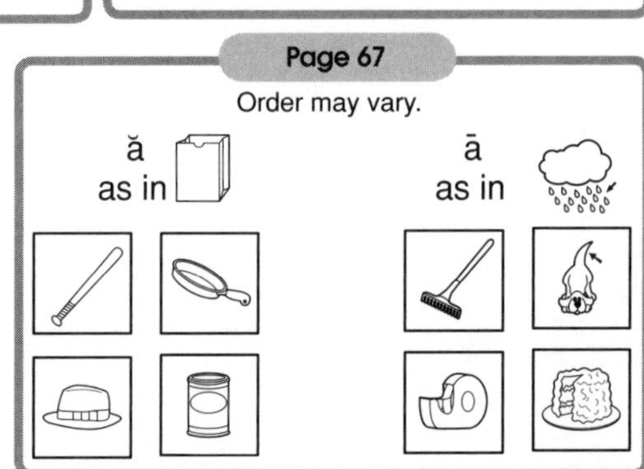

ă as in
ā as in

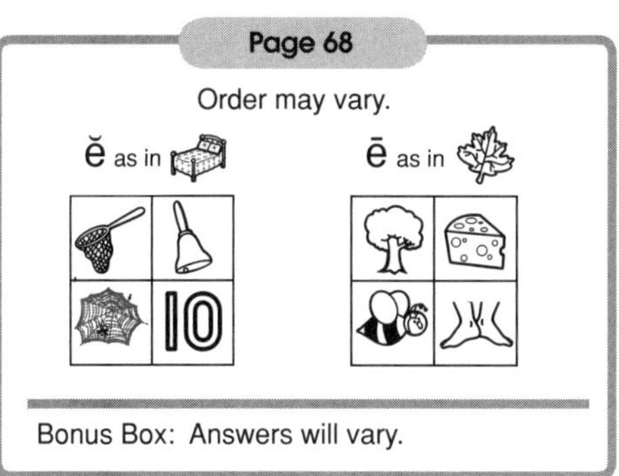
Page 68
Order may vary.
ĕ as in
ē as in
Bonus Box: Answers will vary.

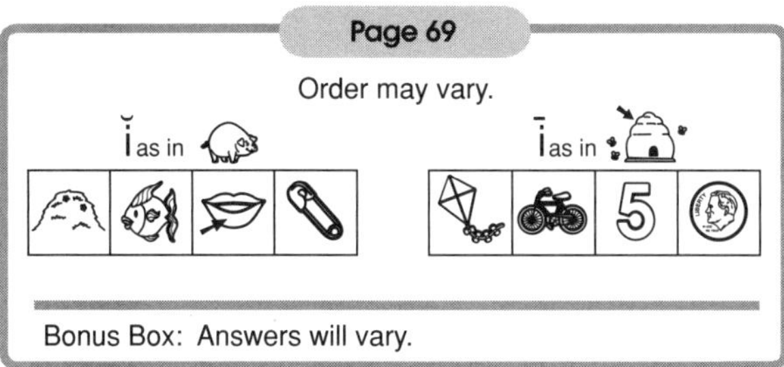
Page 69
Order may vary.
ĭ as in
ī as in
Bonus Box: Answers will vary.

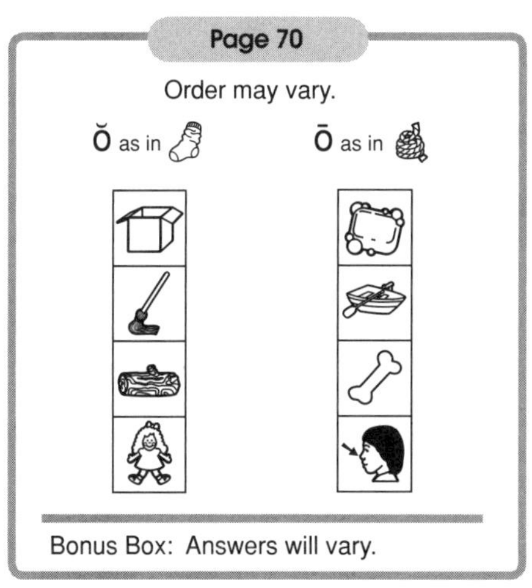
Page 70
Order may vary.
ŏ as in
ō as in
Bonus Box: Answers will vary.

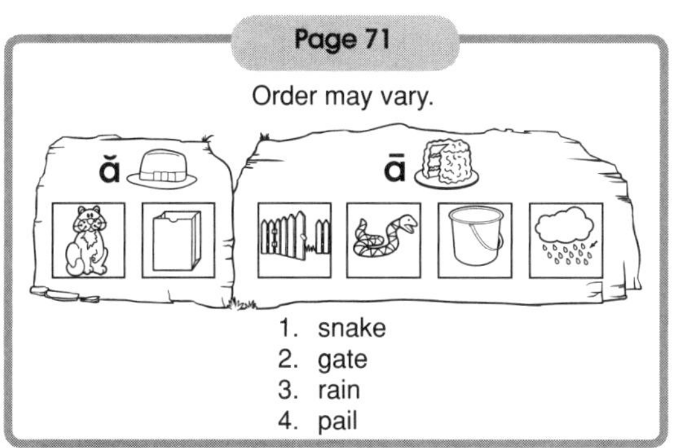
Page 71
Order may vary.
ă
ā
1. snake
2. gate
3. rain
4. pail

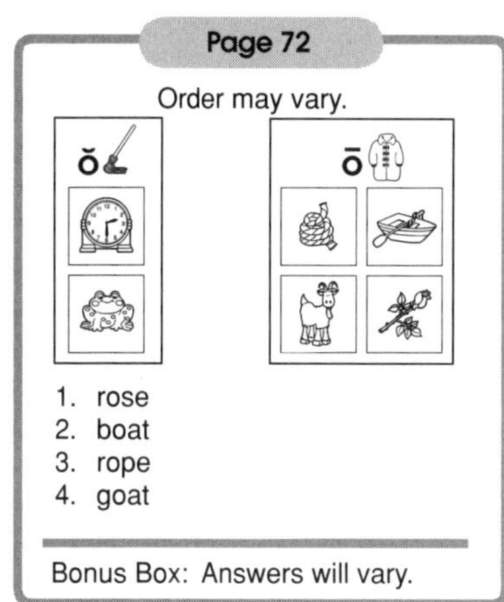
Page 72
Order may vary.
ŏ
ō
1. rose
2. boat
3. rope
4. goat
Bonus Box: Answers will vary.

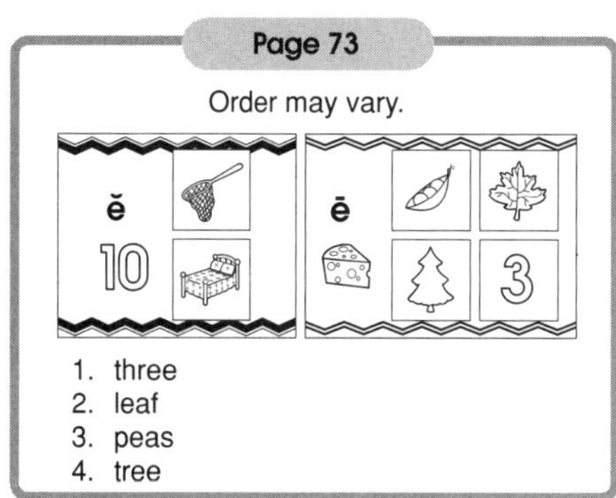
Page 73
Order may vary.
ĕ
ē
1. three
2. leaf
3. peas
4. tree

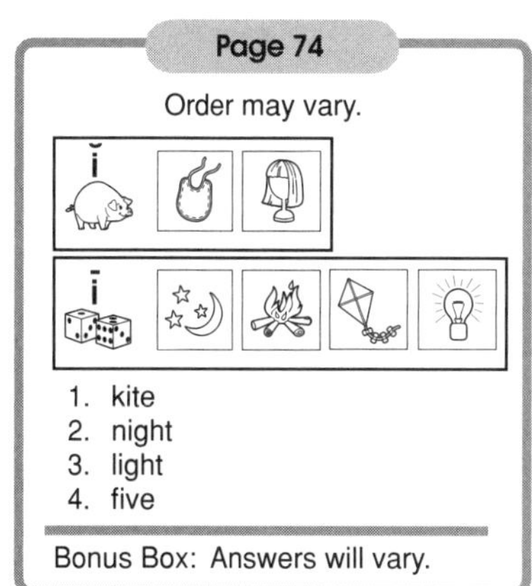
Page 74
Order may vary.
ĭ
ī
1. kite
2. night
3. light
4. five
Bonus Box: Answers will vary.

Page 75
Order may vary.
ch
cheese
chip
chair
sh
shell
sheep
shovel
th 13
thorn
thumb
think

Page 76

Order may vary.

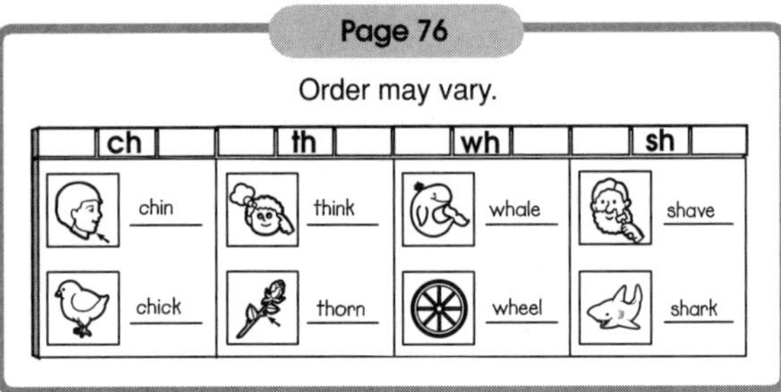

ch
th
wh
sh
chin
think
whale
shave
chick
thorn
wheel
shark

Page 77

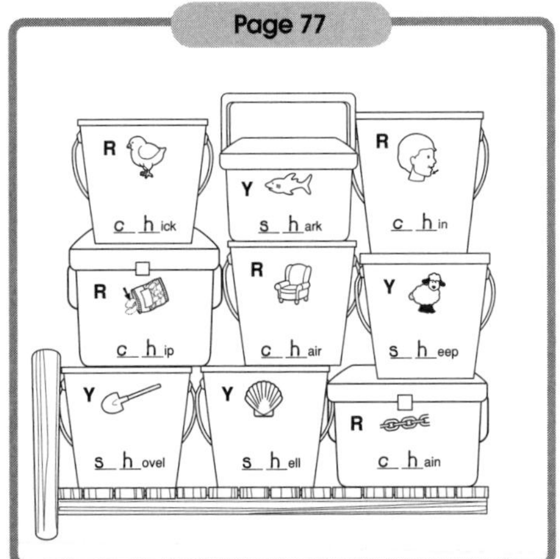

R
c h ick
Y
s h ark
R
c h in
R
c h ip
R
c h air
Y
s h eep
Y
s h ovel
Y
s h ell
R
c h ain

Page 78

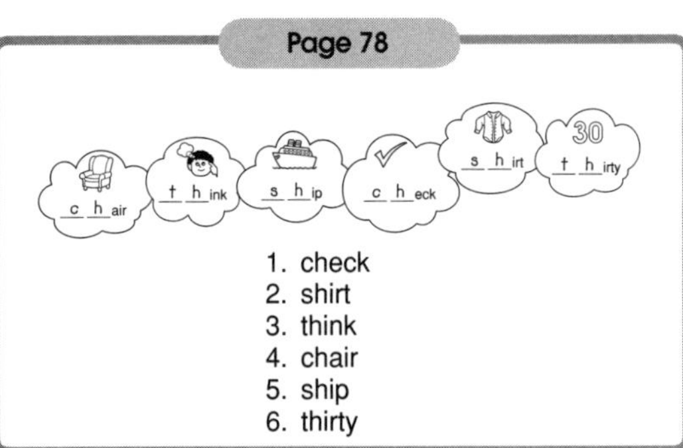

c h air
t h ink
s h ip
c h eck
s h irt
30
t h irty

1. check
2. shirt
3. think
4. chair
5. ship
6. thirty

Page 79

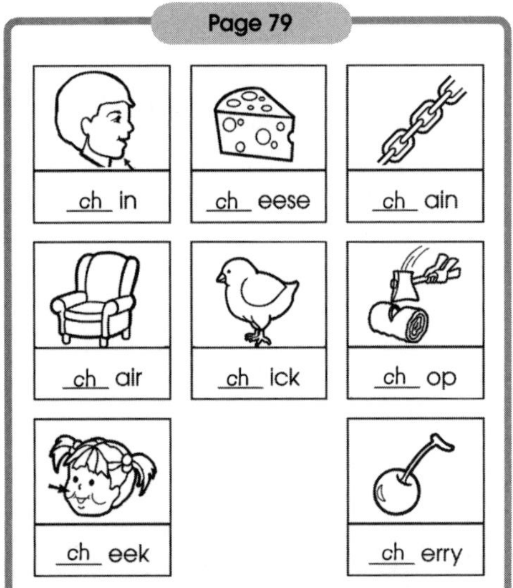

ch in
ch eese
ch ain
ch air
ch ick
ch op
ch eek
ch erry

Page 80

sh ell
sh ave
sh eep
sh ark
sh oe
sh ip
sh irt
sh ovel

Page 81

1. sh (blue)
2. ch (red)
3. th (yellow)
4. sh (blue)
5. th (yellow)
6. sh (blue)
7. sh (blue)
8. ch (red)
9. th (yellow)
10. ch (red)

Bonus Box: Answers will vary.

Page 82

Order may vary.

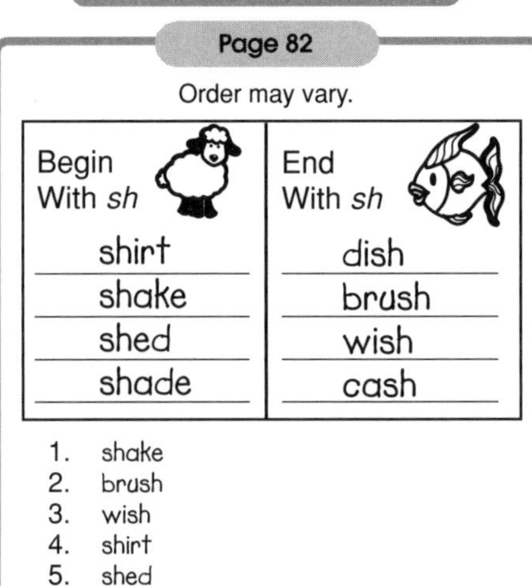

Begin With *sh*	End With *sh*
shirt	dish
shake	brush
shed	wish
shade	cash

1. shake
2. brush
3. wish
4. shirt
5. shed

Bonus Box: Answers will vary.

Page 83

Order may vary.

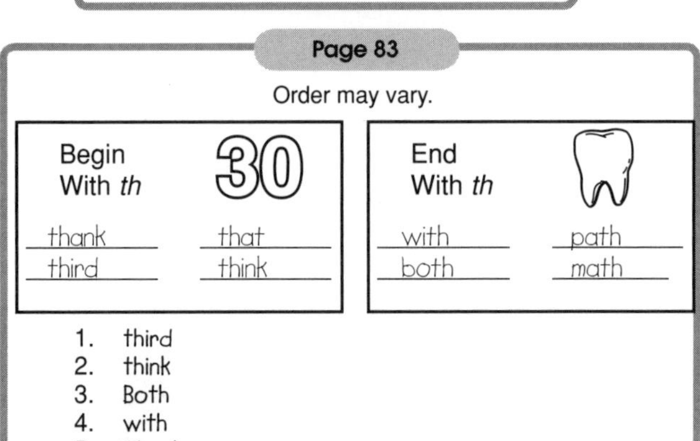

Begin With *th*		End With *th*	
thank	that	with	path
third	think	both	math

1. third
2. think
3. Both
4. with
5. Thank

Page 84

Order may vary.

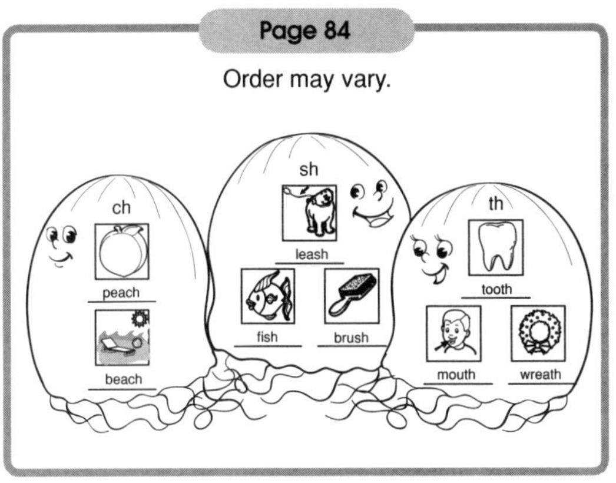

ch
peach
beach
sh
leash
fish
brush
th
tooth
mouth
wreath

Page 85

Order may vary.

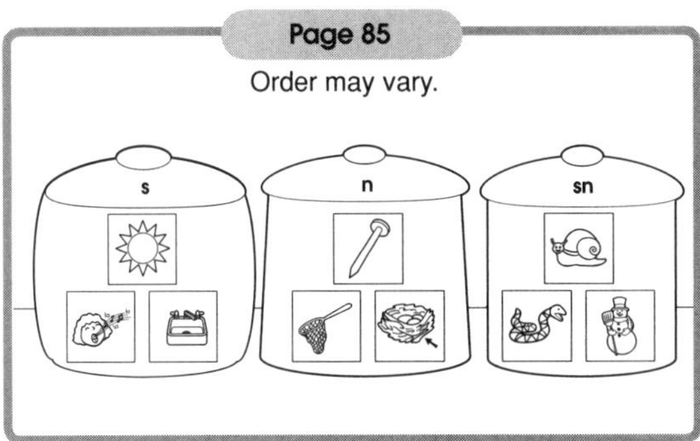

s
n
sn

Page 86

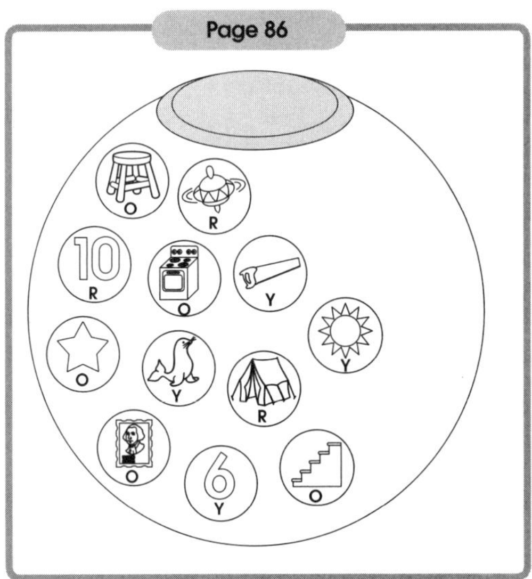

O
R
10
R
O
Y
O
Y
Y
R
O
6
Y
O

Page 87

1. snack
2. store
3. sticks
4. snip
5. spill
6. spot
7. still
8. stay

Page 88

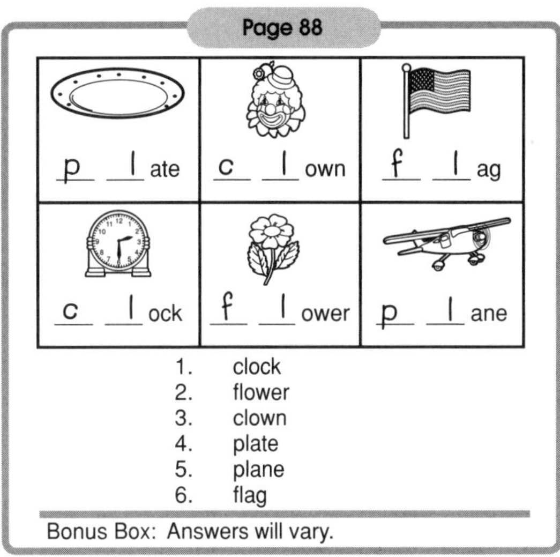

p l ate
c l own
f l ag
c l ock
f l ower
p l ane

1. clock
2. flower
3. clown
4. plate
5. plane
6. flag

Bonus Box: Answers will vary.

Page 89

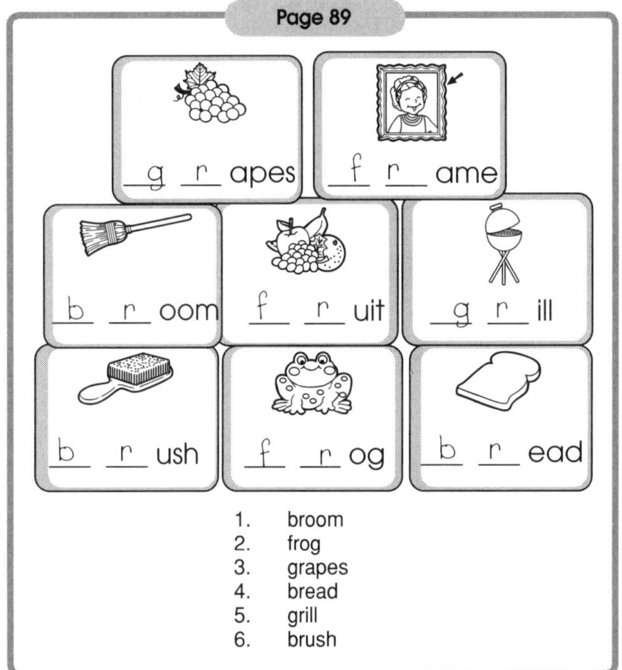

g r apes
f r ame
b r oom
f r uit
g r ill
b r ush
f r og
b r ead

1. broom
2. frog
3. grapes
4. bread
5. grill
6. brush

Page 90

1. plane
2. star
3. flower
4. cloud
5. brush
6. clap
7. snail
8. grapes
9. stump
10. frog
11. spoon
12. plug

Bonus Box: Answers will vary.

Page 91

1. spill
2. stick
3. sponge
4. sky
5. star
6. skillet

Bonus Box: Answers will vary.

Page 92

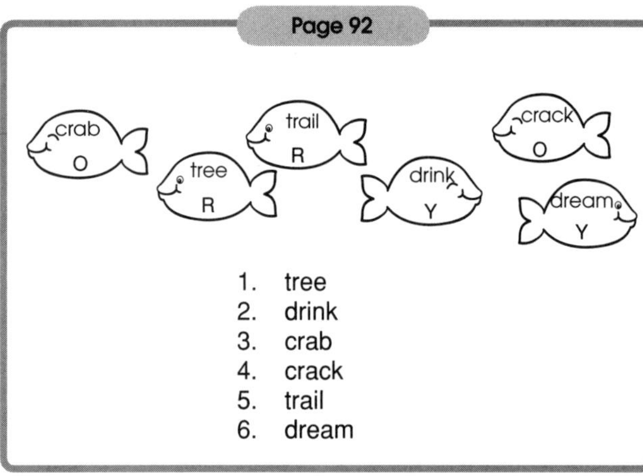

crab
O
tree
R
trail
R
drink
Y
crack
O
dream
Y

1. tree
2. drink
3. crab
4. crack
5. trail
6. dream

Page 93

Order may vary.

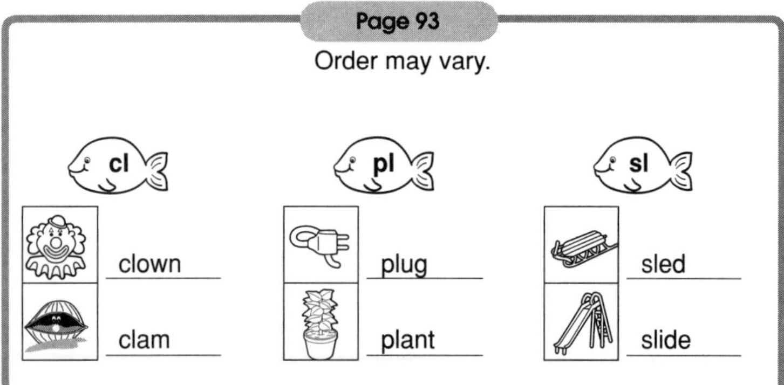

cl
pl
sl
clown
clam
plug
plant
sled
slide

Page 94

Order may vary.

cl
clock
clap
pl
plate
plane
plug
sl
slide
sled
sleep

Page 95

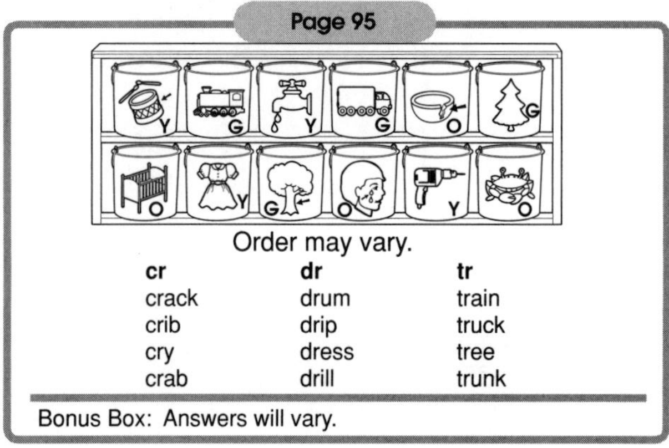

Y
G
Y
G
O
G
O
Y
G
O
Y
O

Order may vary.

cr	dr	tr
crack	drum	train
crib	drip	truck
cry	dress	tree
crab	drill	trunk

Bonus Box: Answers will vary.

Page 96

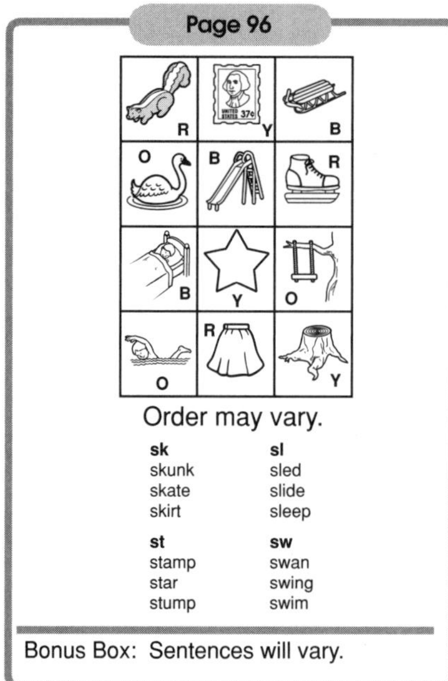

R
Y
B
O
B
R
B
Y
O
O
R
Y

Order may vary.

sk	sl
skunk	sled
skate	slide
skirt	sleep

st	sw
stamp	swan
star	swing
stump	swim

Bonus Box: Sentences will vary.

Page 97

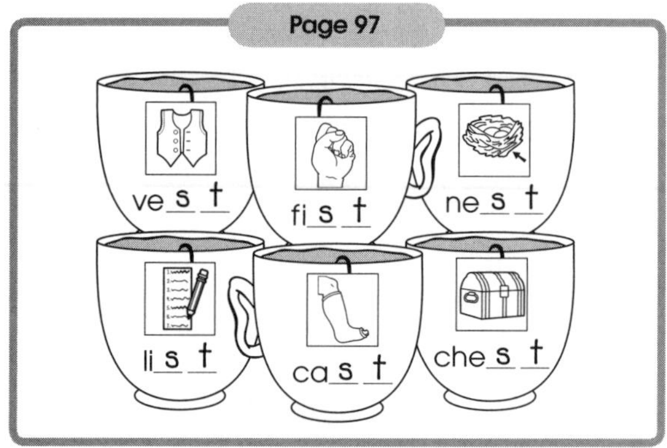

ve s t
fi s t
ne s t
li s t
ca s t
che s t

Page 98

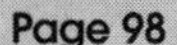

1. list
2. cost
3. fast
4. best
5. must
6. rest
7. vest
8. last

Page 99

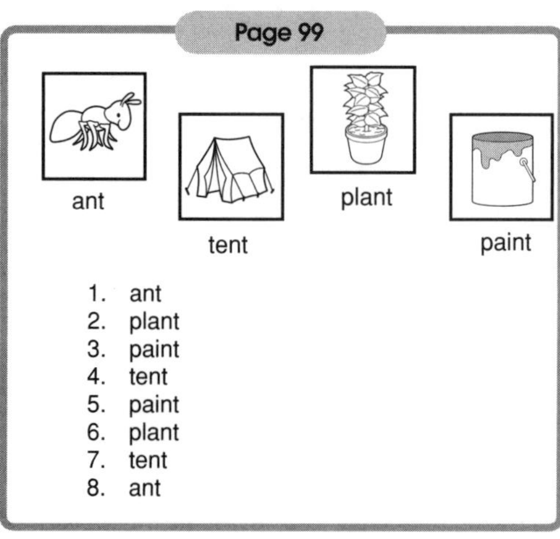

ant
tent
plant
paint

1. ant
2. plant
3. paint
4. tent
5. paint
6. plant
7. tent
8. ant

Page 100

1. went
2. spent
3. sent
4. plant
5. front
6. ant
7. hunt
8. paint

Page 101

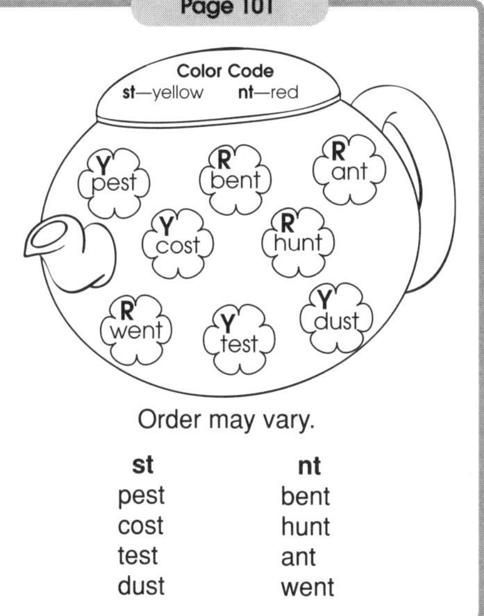

Color Code
st—yellow nt—red
Y pest
R bent
R ant
Y cost
R hunt
R went
Y test
Y dust

Order may vary.

st	nt
pest	bent
cost	hunt
test	ant
dust	went

Page 102

shirt
car
horn
stir
girl
corn
shark
horse
fork
star
bird
yarn

Page 103

1. park
2. far
3. hard
4. star
5. shirt
6. first

Page 104

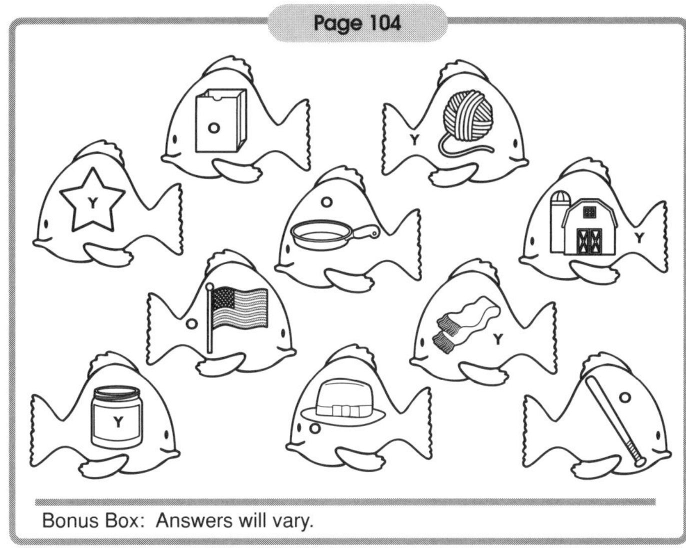

O
Y
Y
Y
O
Y
Y
O

Bonus Box: Answers will vary.

Page 105

Order may vary.

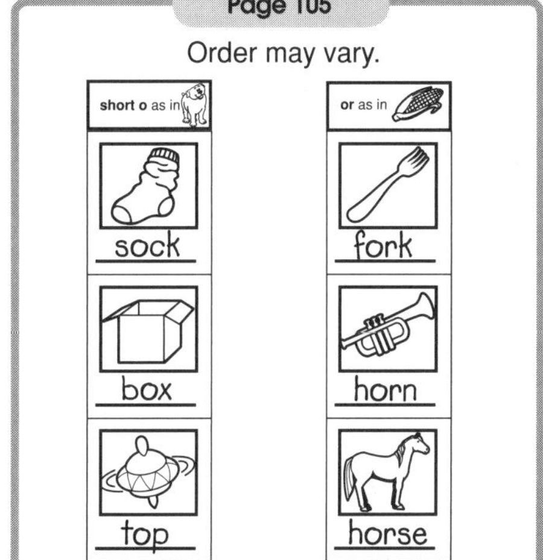

short o as in
or as in
sock
fork
box
horn
top
horse

Bonus Box: Answers will vary.

Page 106

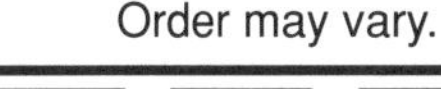

Order may vary.

short i as in
ring
pig
crib
brick

ir as in
shirt
girl
3rd
third
skirt

Page 107

1. her
2. party
3. far
4. water
5. hard
6. after
7. dark
8. summer

Page 108

1. turn
2. far
3. purple
4. hurry
5. cart
6. shark
7. sharp
8. surprise

Bonus Box: Fish with these words should be colored green: *cart, far, shark, sharp.* Fish with these words should be colored purple: *turn, purple, surprise, hurry.*

Page 109

1. star
2. skirt
3. fork
4. turtle
5. corn
6. girl
7. hammer
8. yarn
9. thorn
10. bird
11. turkey
12. ruler

Page 110

soil
sail
jay
joy
boy
bay
bowl
boil
coin
cane
tan
toy

1. toy
2. boy
3. soil
4. joy
5. boil
6. coin

Page 111

1. cowboy
2. enjoy
3. join
4. toy
5. noise
6. point
7. choice
8. foil

Page 112

Order will vary.

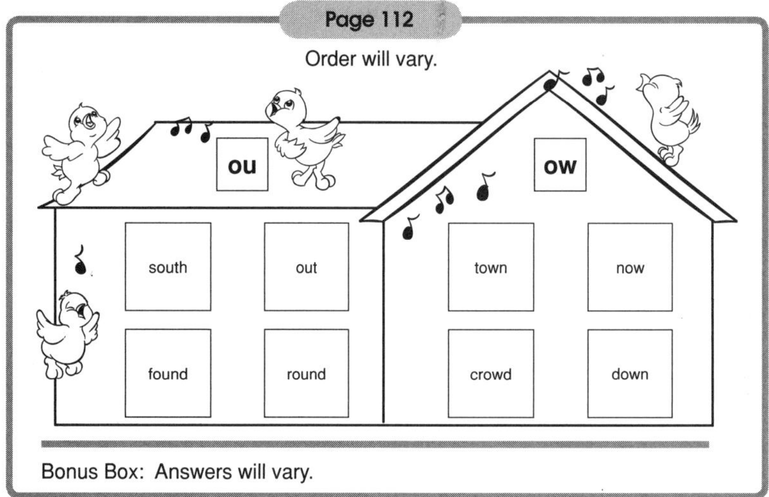

ou
ow
south
out
town
now
found
round
crowd
down

Bonus Box: Answers will vary.

Page 113

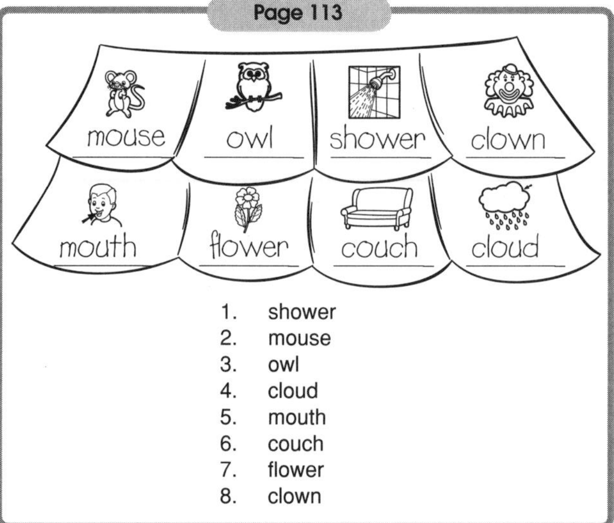

mouse
owl
shower
clown
mouth
flower
couch
cloud

1. shower
2. mouse
3. owl
4. cloud
5. mouth
6. couch
7. flower
8. clown

Page 114

house
mouth
shout
trout
crown
towel
cow

1. crown
2. shout
3. trout
4. towel
5. cow
6. house
7. mouth